PRODUCT POLICY AND MANAGEMENT

Michael J. Baker
Professor of Marketing, University of Strathclyde

Ronald McTavish
Senior Lecturer in Marketing, University of Strathclyde

658.5
B 168

First published 1976 by
THE MACMILLAN PRESS LTD
London and Basingstoke
Associated companies in New York Dublin
Melbourne Johannesburg and Madras

SBN 333 19287 7 (hard cover)
333 19288 5 (paper cover)

Printed in Great Britain by
THE ANCHOR PRESS LTD
Tiptree, Essex

Contents

MACMILLAN STUDIES IN
MARKETING MANAGEMENT

General Editor: Professor Michael J. Baker,
University of Strathclyde

This series is designed to fill the need for a compact treatment of major aspects of marketing management and practice based essentially upon European institutions and experience. This is not to suggest that experience and practice in other advanced economies will be ignored, but rather that the treatment will reflect European custom and attitudes as opposed to American, which has tended to dominate so much of the marketing literature.

Each volume is the work of an acknowledged authority on that subject and combines a distillation of the best and most up-to-date research findings with a clear statement of their relevance to improved managerial practice. A concise style is followed throughout, and extensive use is made of summaries, checklists and references to related work. Thus each work may be viewed as both an introduction to and a reference work on its particular subject. Further, while each book is self-contained, the series as a whole comprises a handbook of marketing management.

The series is designed for both students and practitioners of marketing. Lecturers will find the treatment adequate as the foundation for in-depth study of each topic by more advanced students who have already pursued an introductory and broadly based course in marketing. Similarly, managers will find each book to be both a useful *aide-mémoire* and a reference source.

The first titles in the series are:

International Marketing Management	J. M. Livingstone University of Strathclyde
Pricing	F. Livesey UMIST
Marketing – Theory and Practice	Professor Michael J. Baker University of Strathclyde
Product Policy and Management	Professor Michael J. Baker and Ronald McTavish University of Strathclyde

Preface

The product (and/or service) plays a central role in the activities of all organisations, for it is the medium through which they seek to achieve their dual objectives of maximising both consumer and organisational satisfaction. Thus, while this book is concerned primarily with the management and marketing of the products manufactured by profit-orientated firms, it is believed that many of the principles and policies discussed are of equal relevance to non-profit organisations.

While the book concentrates on managerial problems of product planning and organisation, the product-planning issue is first of all placed in an historical/theoretical setting. On this basis, the main concern with the nature of management problems, and how to overcome them, is pursued. Thus the book has a strong normative interest, namely to develop a practically useful framework of concepts and methods which will be valuable to managements in this vital marketing-mix area.

The broad approach of the book is partly descriptive, partly analytical. In recent years various writers have examined selected aspects of product planning, notably the management of new products, design management, test marketing, and so on. A major objective of this book is to synthesise and unify these into a concise, over-all approach to solving the *total* product-planning problems of the firm. In pursuing this approach we have attempted to impart a practical thrust, seeking realism in our statement of the product-planning problem in its different aspects. The approach is thus directly related to solving real-world business problems. Indeed, much of the material is developed from various live problems the authors have themselves investigated.

In short, the book provides practical guidance on methods for product-planning decision-taking in the firm.

It is addressed to all working managers concerned with such decisions, but will also commend itself to senior managers concerned with the product aspect of corporate strategy. In addition, teachers and students of marketing management will find the book a useful addition to their libraries.

The authors wish to acknowledge not only the many sources cited in the text but also the multiplicity of ideas contributed by both practitioners and academic colleagues which lack a specific reference.

Finally, we would like to record our thanks to our long-suffering secretaries, Miss C. M. Paterson and Mrs M. Murphy, for all their efforts in preparing a legible manuscript, and to our families for their forbearance and encouragement during the writing of it.

Strathclyde University   Michael J. Baker
July 1975   Ronald McTavish

List of Tables

List of Figures

Chapter 1

The Product in Theory and Practice

INTRODUCTION

It is generally accepted among marketing men that their discipline depends heavily upon the economic and behavioural sciences for its theoretical foundations. Because of this dependency it has been suggested that the development of a new discipline of marketing is superfluous in that its subject matter could easily be dealt with within one or other of the disciplines from which it has developed. Naturally, marketers tend to be unsympathetic towards this point of view, and can find considerable support for their lack of sympathy in the subject matter of this book – the product, and product planning and policy.

In this chapter we will attempt to establish that surprisingly little attention has been given to the role of the product in the development of theory in both the economic and behavioural sciences. This lack of emphasis seems surprising when it is appreciated that most forms of human organisation have come into existence in order to provide a product or service to some defined group of customers. (Throughout this book it will be understood that in every case where the term 'product' is used it is interchangeable for 'service'.)

In economics it is postulated that the central economic problem is maximising satisfaction from the consumption of scarce resources. If asked how we should measure the satisfaction derived from the consumption of scarce resources, it seems reasonable to argue that the appropriate criterion is the aggregated satisfaction derived by individual consumers. Although economics tends not to enquire too deeply into the nature of satisfaction at the individual level, being more concerned with aggregated satisfaction, this deficiency is remedied by the interest exhibited in individual consumers by the behavioural sciences. However, economists largely ignore the influence of personal and subjective factors in developing their models of consumption, and the behavioural scientists have so far been unsuccessful in their efforts to develop a theory of aggregated buyer behaviour. It seems to us that one of the main reasons which underlies the emergence of a new area of study identifiable as marketing is due to the fact that the basic disciplines upon which it is founded are loth to trespass in areas which they identify as being the proper concern of the other. Thus neither economics nor the behavioural sciences tends to give much attention to the product itself for reasons which we will explore later in this chapter.

Conversely, the product plays a central role in the subject of marketing – in fact it has been claimed that the whole subject rests upon four cornerstones: product, price, place and promotion. Fundamental to the marketing concept is the belief that good marketing starts and ends with the consumer. Accordingly, normative marketing practice recommends that one should commence by monitoring the nature of consumer needs and then deploy one's resources in the manner which will best satisfy an identified need or needs in a manner consistent with maximising the return on the assets so employed. Clearly, the medium through which the firm attempts to maximise these dual objectives of consumer and corporate satisfaction is the product.

If it could be assumed that consumer needs were unchanging, then clearly it would be possible to develop a fully planned economy in which each producing organisation might be charged with maximising the efficiency of production of a given product or service. However, as is widely recognised, needs change over time and producers must reflect these changing needs if they are to achieve the over-all economic objective of maximising satisfaction.

In a marketing context the reality of this necessity has nowhere been expressed better than in a seminal article written by Ted Levitt and published in 1960.[1] In simple terms,

Levitt's thesis as expounded in this article is that companies often take too narrow a view of the market because they tend to think of it in terms of the product which they are currently supplying rather than in terms of the basic need which that product satisfies. In the course of developing his argument Levitt points out that if the American railroads had conceived of themselves as being in the transportation business then they would not have ignored the competitive threat implicit in the development of the internal combustion engine. Rather, they would have appreciated that the internal combustion engine offered an alternative method of satisfying the basic human need for transportation and would have taken steps to develop an integrated transport system which would have built upon the benefits of the steam locomotive and the motor-car and lorry. In turn, with the development of aeroplanes, a firm with a concept of its business as being transportation would have adopted this innovation and become a fully integrated transport firm.

Whereas basic needs tend to remain fairly constant over time – as is implicit in Maslow's need hierarchy[2] – means of satisfying these needs are subject to continuous change. Fundamentally, change occurs because of competition between rivals seeking to secure control over an increased share of available resources. In that most resources are in fixed supply in the short term, and in finite supply even in the long term, efforts of any single organisation to improve its size and influence can only be achieved by a corresponding reduction in the size and influence of some other organisation or organisations. In turn, the success of an organisation is determined in the market-place where it sells the goods or services which constitute its output. It follows, therefore, that individual preferences for specific goods and services (products) are the ultimate determinants of the structure of economies and of the relative success enjoyed by the organisations within these economies.[3]

We turn now to a more detailed examination of the role of the product in theory and practice.

THE PRODUCT IN ECONOMIC THEORY

In the introduction to the first chapter of his thought-provoking book, *Quality and Competition*, Lawrence Abbott points out that

> the core of theoretical economies has been, from the time of Ricardo and Cournot up to the present Keynesian age, the theory of competitive markets; and the kind of competition envisaged in this theory has been the kind that occurred in the great produce markets, where many buyers and sellers bicker over the terms of sale of quantities of some homogeneous or standardised commodity whose quality is never called into question. . . . One rather striking feature about such markets is the complete absence – at least from the picture as presented in economic analysis – of quality difference, quality variations and hence of quality comparisons.[4]

As Abbott goes on to point out, if one eliminates quality differences from consideration then the conditions which define such a market also define the single kind of competition which may occur in it, namely price competition. At the time when the classical economists were evolving their theory of pure or perfect competition, by which was automatically understood competition on the basis of price, the economies of Western Europe and the United States were undergoing radical changes due to the impact of the Industrial Revolution. By virtue of the mass production techniques brought into existence by the development of a factory system, product homogeneity was probably more of a reality in the late eighteenth and nineteenth centures than it had ever been hitherto, or is likely to be again. One does not need to be an historian to appreciate that higher levels of employment, increased disposable income and parallel advances in public health all combined to produce a rapidly expanding population hungry for basic goods and services. Under these conditions it is unsurprising that producers should emphasise quantity rather than quality or choice, and hence may be categorised as production-orientated. To this extent the classical economist's neglect of product differences is partially excusable.

However, by the end of the nineteenth century the advanced industrialised economies were approaching a stage of near saturation in terms of consumption of basic goods and services. Further, during the second half of the nineteenth century, the more efficient producers had grown at the expense of their less efficient rivals with the result that one of the basic propositions or assumptions for the existence of perfect competition no longer applied, namely that no individual producer controlled a sufficient volume of supply to any given market such that they could radically affect the total supply to that market.

Because of the concentration of supply in the hands of a relatively few producers (oligopolists) in many markets it soon became apparent that competition on the basis of price could easily become self-defeating. In part this was attributable to the fact that the survivors of the preceding period of price competition had generally achieved a size where further economies of scale in production and distribution were no longer open to them. Thus, in a situation where further cost savings were not possible through increased sales volume, any attempt to achieve greater market share through price reductions would inevitably lead to a lower unit margin. Further, in that loss of sales due to price cutting by a rival would result in an increase in unit cost and therefore a reduced margin on a falling sales volume, such a producer would be likely to react to price cutting with an equivalent reduction of his own. Clearly the net effect of such price competition is to reduce the margins available to all suppliers which, in the long run, will result in lower profits, lower investment and eventual decline into stagnation or worse. Under such circumstances it is unsurprising that oligopolistic producers should choose not to compete on the basis of price but should prefer to pursue a policy of product differentiation.

By the early years of the twentieth century the more percipient economists had recognised that such a change had taken place and that product differentiation was more typically the basis of competition than was price. In the early 1930s this view was crystallised in two famous contributions by Joan

Robinson and Edward Chamberlin.[5] While it was rapidly accepted that non-price competition reflected reality, this recognition did little to change attitudes towards the basic belief that price competition is preferable. It follows that if price competition is to be endowed with the description 'perfect' or 'pure', then non-price competition by definition must be imperfect or impure. Thus, as Abbott notes, 'market situations of the real world which deviate from pure competition must be considered 'inferior' and acceptance of imperfect competition as the normal case 'has not been to dethrone pure competition, but simply to transfer its position of that of the *typical* competitive situation to that of the *ideal* competitive situation'.

As Abbott proceeds to demonstrate with great clarity and precision, while the concept of pure competition has great utility as a tool of analysis in dealing with many specific economic problems it is unrealistic to consider it as the standard or normal situation. In consequence, Abbott points out that 'economic theory must somehow find room for the idea that product differentiation and variation form an integral part and desirable feature of any conceivable kind of exchange economy. The first step is to reject the "perfectly competitive system" as a standard of evaluation.'

One possible explanation for the failure of many economists to allow for quality variations in their models is their unwillingness to admit of variations in human behaviour other than to term them 'irrational' when they depart from the economic norms for rationality. Fortunately, while economists tend to ignore behavioural influences, and in turn behavioural scientists tend to play down the influence of economic factors, the marketing man is prepared to draw on both disciplines in developing a workable understanding of the nature and extent of consumer preferences for differentiated products.

PRODUCT DIFFERENTIATION

We have already pointed out that in the early stages of the Industrial Revolution development of mass-production tech-

niques was associated with a high degree of product homogeneity. Such homogeneity may be considered the result of
two factors; first, uniformity in the output of any individual
manufacturer due to standardisation of the material inputs and
process by which such inputs were fabricated, and second, the
absence of any significant premium for a differentiated product in the market-place itself. However, the more nearly the
total supply can match the total demand for a basic product
then the more significant it becomes to any individual supplier
that he should be able to distinguish his output from that
of his competitors as a basis for developing preference for his
output.

In the early stages of developing a differentiated product it
seems likely that the basis for differentiation was more intuitive than based upon any serious attempt to distinguish between variations in the needs of different groups of consumers
and a conscious attempt to develop products to cater for these
needs. In other words, the producer would develop a differentiated product and then infer the characteristics of his customers by an analysis of those actually buying the product.
Today, a marketing-orientated firm would tend to approach the
question of developing a differentiated product from the
starting-point that all consumers differ from each other to some
degree. In the final analysis, therefore, every single individual
may be regarded as a market segment.[6] However, for most
practical purposes the one-off production of items tailored to
the precise needs of the individual is grossly uneconomic.
Accordingly, in segmenting a market one is more usually concerned with establishing broad differences than with pursuing
such differences to an ultimate conclusion. Pragmatically the
aim is to identify a group of consumers of sufficient size to
make it profitable to develop a product which caters to their
highly specific needs. Clearly the benefit if one is successful is
that one possesses a monopoly over the differentiating factor.
In turn this enables one to earn above-average profits and enjoy
a captive market for one's output.

Although the term 'monopolistic competition' coined by
Chamberlin appears at first sight to be a contradiction in logic,
it is an accurate description of the situation in most oligopolistic markets at a given point in time. Thus, if one were to

analyse the behaviour of firms in such a market one could easily come to the conclusion that all are enjoying the benefits of a monopoly over their own output. In the short term it is possible that this is perfectly true, although it seems more likely that some products will be enjoying increasing success while others are declining in importance. However, as we have already noted earlier, conditions change over time and the firm must continuously monitor the satisfaction derived by their customers as well as the alternative satisfactions offered to them by competitors.

The reasons why there is continuous change in the nature of goods demanded is summed up in a nutshell by Abbott when he states that 'what people really desire are not the products but satisfying experiences'. Further, he goes on to say that 'experiences are attained through activities. In order that activities may be carried out, physical objects or the services of human beings are usually needed. Here lies the connecting link between man's inner world and the outer world of economic activity. People want products because they want the experience-bringing services which they hope the products will render.'

People's desire for satisfying experiences are pungently summarised in two frequently quoted statements. The first by Ralph Waldo Emerson contends that 'If a man build a better mouse-trap, even though he live in a wood, the world will beat a path to his door.' While modern-day marketers quarrel with the accuracy of this statement on the grounds that if the existence of the better mouse-trap is unknown then no one will be able to express a preference for it, let alone beat a path to the door of its manufacturer. Accordingly, the modern marketing concept recognises that it is not sufficient merely to manufacture a better product; it is also necessary to bring it to the attention of would-be consumers. Assuming, however, that potential users of mouse-traps are made aware of the existence of a better mouse-trap, then rationality demands that they will prefer it.

Our second quotation is attributed to Charles Revson who commented that 'In the factory we make cosmetics, and in the drug store we sell hope.' The implication is clear. Cosmetics have little or no intrinsic value in themselves and are only desired for the satisfactions which they can confer, most of which are probably more subjective than objective.

While it was once contended that there is a fundamental difference between the marketing of industrial and consumer goods, on the basis that the industrial buyer was motivated solely by objective criteria, while the ultimate consumer was guided more by subjective criteria, it is now generally accepted that all buying behaviour contains elements of both. Irrespective of their status, all buyers would seem to demand that a prospective purchase should satisfy certain minimum performance criteria and offer such a performance within a specified price bracket. In most competitive markets it will usually be found that several products will meet these economic criteria and still leave the potential buyer with a need to choose between a number of competing alternatives. At this juncture it is unsurprising that subjective preferences will influence the final choice whether it be of a machine tool or a bar of soap. In both cases the buyer is seeking to satisfy a known need and will evaluate the degree to which the chosen purchase does in fact satisfy that need. If, subsequently, an alternative is brought to his attention which possesses some feature that he has found to be deficient in his previous purchase, then once again reason dictates that the new product will be preferred when the buyer is next in the market for supplies of a similar description.

It is often argued that, by virtue of a policy of product differentiation, and as a result of industrial concentration, the ensuing state of monopolistic competition will in fact be characterised by the absence of competition. In all but a very limited number of cases such an assumption is generally wrong. Because consumers are continuously seeking new and better ways of satisfying their needs, producers find it necessary continuously to improve their product merely to stay in business. In the short term any significant improvement is likely to result in a transference in demand to the improved product, leading to a predictable reaction by competitors to either emulate or improve upon this more preferred offering.

It also seems true that most companies aspire to increase their market share and grow in size and influence. It is somewhat ironical that companies only become sensitive about their size when they approach the arbitrary market share which most economies stipulate constitutes an official monopoly. Once a company approaches or surpasses the stipulated market share – 25 per cent in the United Kingdom – manufacturers frequently become conscious that they are conspicuous and so cease to strive for further increases in sales. In this respect monopoly and anti-trust legislation can act as a real dampener on competition and can become an excuse for the continued survival of inefficient companies which otherwise might be pushed out of existence by their more efficient competitors. (In the United States, it is generally recognised that the big three motor-car manufacturers – General Motors, Ford and Chrysler – have refrained from pushing American Motors out of business for fear of the unwelcome publicity which such an action would have.)

In the long run, however, competitive forces tend to reassert themselves. Thus while the big three U.S. motor-car manufactuers might refrain from putting American Motors out of business they can hardly have been said to have taken a non-competitive approach towards the activities of, first Volkswagen, and later the Japanese, both of whom have succeeded in pre-empting a significant share of the total U.S. automobile market by offering a differentiated product more in keeping with an energy-conscious economy of the 1970s. (We consider the role of product policy in the U.S. automobile industry in some detail in the final chapter.)

In fact, observation suggests that there is a remarkable consistency in the stages through which products pass from invention to obsolescence. The regularity of this pattern has given rise to the statement of a concept which we examine in greater detail in the following section.

THE PRODUCT LIFE-CYCLE CONCEPT

As suggested earlier, observation of the sales history of successful new products exhibits a remarkable consistency. It has been suggested that this consistency is indicative of an underlying natural process the inevitability of which can be appreciated by consideration of the life cycle of living organisms.[7] Such consideration suggests that after a period of gestation most organisms pass through a period of rapid growth until they reach a stage of maturity. On achievement of maturity the organism exhibits only limited and marginal changes for a period which is usually longer than that taken to achieve maturity. Ultimately, however, a decline sets in which, in the case of a living organism, culminates in death.

By analogy, the concept of the product life cycle postulates that the new product will pass through an introductory period

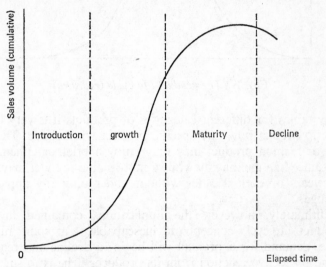

FIG. 1.1 *The product life cycle*

followed by rapid growth leading to maturity and decline. Diagramatically, this cycle is usually represented by an S-shaped curve similar to that reproduced as Figure 1.1. Such a curve is derived by plotting cumulative sales against elapsed time from introduction. Less often this same data is represented by plotting unit sales for a standardised period of time when the result will appear as a normal or near-normal distribution as reproduced in Figure 1.2.

The great value of the product life-cycle concept is its emphasis upon the stages through which all products must pass. Its major deficiency is that in the absence of any life-expect-

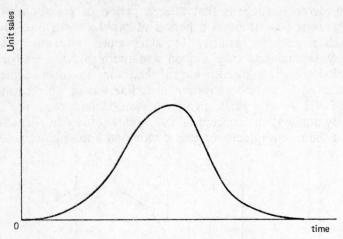

FIG. 1.2 *The product life cycle (redrawn)*

ancy tables for different categories of products it is very difficult to predict how any specific product will behave. Thus a
fad or fashion product may only enjoy a brief or ephemeral
existence like the may fly while a more stable product may last
for years or even decades without undergoing any apparent
change.

Ultimately, however, the implications contained in the
product life-cycle concept are inescapable – at some future
time, demand for a product will begin to decline and require
some protective reaction from its producer if he is to survive.
It is because of uncertainty as to when such a decline will begin
to make itself felt that most producers devote a considerable
portion of their energies to planning product modifications or
changes as an insurance against a decline of interest in their
existing product or products.

Because of such competitive pressures new product intro-
ductions account for an increasing proportion of both the sales
and profits of many producers in competitive markets. Hard
data as to the extent of this dependency are difficult to come
by, but Figures 1.3 and 1.4 are felt to be reasonably representative of the position for consumer and industrial goods.[8]

While Figures 1.3 and 1.4 indicate the importance of new
products to the firm, they give no indication of the risk and

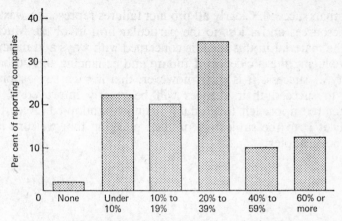

FIG. 1.3 Consumer-goods manufacturers' dependence on new products (50 companies reporting)

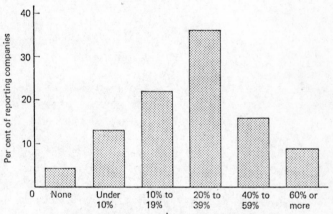

FIG. 1.4 Industrial-goods manufacturers' dependence on new products (173 companies reporting)

opportunities implicit in new product development. We return to the issue several times later in this book, but at this juncture it will be useful to make the point that most informed observers would subscribe to the view that more new products fail than succeed. Clearly all product failures represent a waste of resources and a loss to the particular firm involved. Much of the material in this book is concerned with ways and means of reducing the incidence of failure and enhancing the probability of success. It is clear, however, that if such suggestions are to succeed their chances will be greatly improved if a structured approach to product planning is adopted. Accordingly it is to the subject of product planning that we turn in the next chapter.

Chapter 2

Product Planning

INTRODUCTION

In this chapter we attempt to define, first, what product planning is and, secondly, its relationship to the over-all strategy
of the firm. Having identified the role which product planning
has to play within the over-all marketing strategy, we then
turn to an examination of product policies as a guide to product planning. Such consideration leads naturally to a review
of different approaches and the problems associated with these.
Recognising that product planning is not a universal activity
within all organisations, we then review some of the reasons
for its neglect prior to looking at those situations where it is
most likely to be present, namely in programmes for the
development of new products. We conclude by surveying
alternative methods of organising for product planning and
new-product development before concluding with some
generalisations on the activity as a whole.

THE MEANING AND SCOPE OF PRODUCT PLANNING

The term 'product planning' is used by a variety of organisations to denote a wide range of activities. In manufacturing
firms the term is frequently used as if it were interchangeable
with 'new-product development process'. However, while new
product development frequently constitutes a major element
of the product-planning process, to confine planning merely
to its new product development component can be dangerously
misleading.

Product planning deals with the product mix or assortment

of products offered by an organisation. A useful definition of product planning, felt to be equally applicable in both the industrial and consumer context, was contained in a recently published survey of the machine-tool industry,[1] namely: 'Evaluation of the range, mix, specification and pricing of existing and new products in relation to present and future market requirements and competition; planning of product range, mix, specification and pricing to satisfy company objectives; and specifying the research, design and development support required.' From this definition it is clear that both existing and potential products must be included in the product-planning activity, and it follows that the activity itself should deal with the proper balance between old and new products in the product-mix in so far as the future course of the business is concerned. The evaluation and planning activities referred to, and particularly the emphasis on satisfying the company's objectives, implies the existence of an over-all corporate plan which provides a framework within which these activities may take place.

TOP MANAGEMENT'S CONTRIBUTION TO THE PRODUCT-PLANNING PROCESS

In the preceding chapter we argued that the importance of the product or service lies in the fact that it is the medium through which scarce resources are allocated to different ends in response to expressed consumer preferences. Thus, if the purpose of economies is to allocate scarce resources so as to maximise satisfaction, then consideration of the nature of products must play a central part in any evaluation of the effectiveness of economies. It was also argued that consumer preferences are dynamic, not static, and so require continual adjustment in the nature of product offerings in response to changes in consumer preferences.

In a free-enterprise, market economy firms compete with one another for a share of the available factors of production. Ultimately, their success in securing supplies of these factors is dependent upon their ability to transform these factors into saleable products. The more successful they are in specifying customer needs and developing products to satisfy them, then the greater the demand for their products and the greater their opportunity to earn money surpluses as a reward for their efforts. Clearly, the larger the surplus or profit, the greater the control the firm can exercise over securing supplies of new factor inputs.

In this century a better understanding of the relationship between a clearly defined appreciation of consumer needs and the ultimate profitability of the firm had led to the emergence of a marketing orientation as the dominant managerial philosophy. In its simplest form a marketing orientation requires that a firm sets out to identify and measure consumer preferences as a basis for deploying the resources over which it has control, in a manner which will maximise the value added to the use of those resources. In this process top management's function is to identify the nature of the business which it is in and wishes to be in, and to decide the basic objectives for the firm including (1) the new markets it would like to exploit; (2) the growth rate which it is to achieve in terms of sales, profit, personnel and production capacity; (3) the rate of return on investment or other financial criteria; and (4) any other more specific goals which it may desire. Once such goals are articulated, realistic policies for all the activities of the business can be formulated including product planning. A suggested checklist of questions which top management may be asked to answer in formulating corporate objectives is presented in Table 2.1.

The product-mix offered has a direct bearing upon the future of the company, for if it is unsatisfactory to its customers the inevitable outcome will be losses and, ultimately, failure. On the other hand, a product-mix which satisfies customer demand goes a long way towards ensuring the financial health and growth of the firm.

Thus, within the over-all corporate plan as set down by senior management, the product plan usually represents the activity which links the company with its market, and so is most directly concerned with the forward development of the company as a whole. This is not to say that product planning is the prerogative of top management, indeed it is a function which is most usually discharged by line management, but

TABLE 2.1

Checklist for setting long-range corporate objectives

1. What business are we in?
2. Where is our market? Who are our customers?
3. What business do we want to be in five years from now – ten years from now?
4. What immediate problems must we solve? Which ones are so critical that their solution, in one way or another, will have an important influence on the future of our firm?
5. What should be our return on investment three years from now? in five years? in ten years?
6. What image of our corporation is conveyed to its various publics? Is it what we want? Can we change what we do not want?
7. What personnel policies do we practise and what policies do we want to follow in the future? Have we clearly worked out our approaches, for example, to automation and labour; middle-management executive development?
8. How big do we want to be – three, five, ten years from now? What should be our annual rate of growth?
9. What share of the market do we want for each of our product lines – three, five, ten years from now?
10. What means should we use to grow – acquisition, merger, research and development, improved marketing?
11. How shall we finance growth?
12. What should we do to strengthen our position in international markets?

Source: Bruce Payne, *Planning for Company Growth* (New York: McGraw-Hill, 1963).

rather to argue that successful product planning can only occur within a clear framework of goals and objectives laid down by the board of directors. Further, senior management must ensure direct lines of communication between itself and the product-planning function.

PRODUCT POLICIES AND PRODUCT OBJECTIVES AS GUIDES TO PRODUCT PLANNING

The main function of product policy is to guide the activities of the firm towards common goals. In that the success of the company is measured not only by its current profits but also by its long-term growth, the company must strike a delicate balance between optimising its current operations and making adequate provision for the future. In a manufacturing concern, or any other organisation for that matter, these aims can best be reconciled through a continuity of product policy.

Major product questions upon which product policies bear, include: the importance of the product-mix in the firm's overall marketing strategy; the rate, nature and direction of changes in demand for existing products and its implications for product elimination and new product development decisions; the product policy of its competitors, and so on. Product policies do not provide the answers to these and other product-line questions, but help to suggest the relative emphasis and balance which should be given to each. In addition they do provide guidelines for efficient planning and action. In a survey of machine-tool manufacturing companies,[2] successful companies were found to have strong commitment to the attainment of leadership in the field in which they operated. Recognising the impossibility of being a leader in all areas, such companies have accepted that their resources in design, production and selling give them a competitive advantage in certain areas, and so they concentrate their efforts on these. The result is clearly formulated product policies enabling the most successful manufacturers to channel their planning activities into areas offering the best prospects of success. In this way, business objectives, through the medium of product policies, influence the future course of a company.

PRODUCT PLANNING AND MARKETING STRATEGY

In the first chapter we noted that the product is one of four cornerstones upon which the marketing edifice has been erected. It follows, therefore, that product policy must be in-extricably linked with the firm's over-all marketing strategy. Thus, while the focus of this book is on the product, this variable can never be wholly separated from the other three variables – price, place and promotion. The optimum com-bination of these four variables is the continuing and over-riding concern of marketing management. In practice it is doubtful if an optimum solution can ever be attained due to the multiplicity and dynamic nature of the variables involved. In theory, of course, if a firm defines its sole objective as profit maximisation, then an optimum combination of the four variables may be achieved by equalising the marginal re-turns for each of them. Of course, in practice, marginal returns are exceedingly difficult to calculate to any degree of accuracy and at worst may be unknown. This is not to say that the company must either resort to trial-and-error methods or depend solely on subjective judgement. Several useful solutions to the problem have been proposed which can accommodate complex relationships involving many variables including the use of desert-and-oasis charts. This approach to the selection of optimum marketing mixes was formulated by P. J. Verdoorn[3] and comprises a formal expression of a technique available to firms confronted with a complex assortment of marketing variables.

Given a particular product and its price, the company's first decision is to determine which marketing techniques appear relevant – that is to whom the product can be sold and what methods will induce potential customers to buy it. Once this decision has been made the next stage requires an evaluation of the total cost of different combinations of the marketing inputs required to market the product. Included in this calcula-tion are values for each of the instruments that compose the particular mix. Estimates are made of the quantity of advert-ising and personal selling, the distribution methods, and the product characteristics necessary to sell a given quantity of output. The cost of each of these inputs is aggregated thus pro-viding a point estimate – that is a single value – for each likely input. These point estimates (oases) are then plotted on a revenue–cost/output chart (the desert). Each point represents the total cost (measured along the vertical axis of a particular marketing-mix. The oases are plotted on the horizontal axis above the output (sales) that they are expected to produce.

Figure 2.1 shows a desert-and-oasis chart for seven marketing-mixes. The scatter of oases represents the cost function, the straight line represents the revenue function, and M_1, M_2, ... M_7 represent the various mixes. The broken line sketched

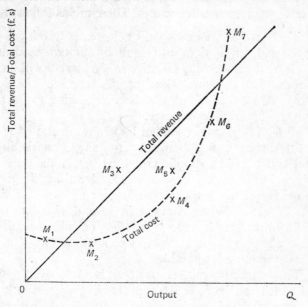

FIG. 2.1 *Desert-and-oasis map for selected marketing-mixes*

through those oases provides the lowest costs for given outputs, Q. By identifying the oasis that is furthest below the revenue curve – M_4 – the company is in a position to locate the maximum-profit position, and hence the optimum marketing-mix. Such points as M_1, M_3 and M_7, which lie above the revenue curve, are obviously relatively inefficient mixes. The use of a smooth cost curve in the diagram is merely for convenience. In practice it is likely to be anything but smooth.

While this approach is of value in expressing in a formal way the procedures employed by many firms, its usefulness is severely limited by the accuracy which can be brought into the relevant calculations. As stated above, marginal analysis is of very restricted applicability because of the difficulty of assessing the revenue consequences of varying particular elements in the mix. How much more complex, therefore, is the problem of determining the likely profitability of one entire mix as against several others.

The problems of quantification in this area can be further highlighted by considering some of the uncertainties inherent in selecting a given marketing-mix. These are as follows:

(1) The several marketing-mix elements (product, price, channels and promotion) are mutually interdependent; no single element can be fully effective in the market without support from other elements. Thus planners need to consider the full range of marketing-mix elements in seeking to formulate an integrated marketing strategy.

(2) Marketing planners seldom have any precise knowledge about the relationship between any single marketing-mix element and sales in a specific target market. In the case of advertising, for example, estimates of advertising impact on sales are frequently imprecise and must allow for a sizable margin of error. When changes in several elements of the marketing-mix are in prospect (the normal situation in strategic planning), the problem of estimating effects on sales becomes even more formidable.

(3) The marketing-mix is planned for use over a future period which can be forecast in probabilistic terms only.

(4) The planned marketing-mix should not exceed the physical, financial and managerial capabilities of the company.

Because of such conditions, managements are rarely certain they have planned the optimal marketing-mix to reach desired market goals. Uncertainty is present in all planning decisions. Even market testing or the actual execution of the market plan cannot be depended upon to demonstrate whether the marketing-mix is the optimal one, although it may show whether the mix is defective and, possibly, how it may be improved. To say that companies should have *the* optimal marketing-mix, let alone have detailed knowledge of the effectiveness of several mixes, is a counsel of perfection. The advantage of planning lies in its rational approach to marketing-mix decisions in full recognition of their many problems and uncertainties. Only by recognising these problems can managements hope to overcome or minimise them. By striving to improve the marketing-mix in the face of numerous uncertainties planners have the expectation of developing a more effective set of market policies than a company whose policies are not grounded on conscious deliberation. Such an advantage could constitute the decisive advantage in competitive markets.

In the next chapter we deal with the basic product strategies which are open to a firm. It is from the statement of such strategies that specific policies may be determined and laid down which, in turn, may lead to the selection of particular techniques, as was described above, for determining the best mix for executing a given product policy. However, all this presumes that firms are convinced of the desirability of setting up a formal product-planning system. In reality many firms, especially those in fairly stable markets, are not convinced of the need for a formal product-planning function. Further, as we have already noticed in some companies, product planning is equated with new-product development and so considered an unnecessary luxury by the firm whose basic product line has experienced little change in recent years. Alternatively, product planning may not be identified as an essential corporate activity, but may be relegated to the position of a subfunction of the R and D or production department.

These points are well exemplified in the findings of a study undertaken by Cunningham and Hammouda which examined the practices of seven large engineering companies in the United Kingdom.[4] In two cases, product planning is not being undertaken in any recognisable form: in four cases the concept of product planning has not been 'translated into action', and only in one case has product planning been adopted in a comprehensive manner. However, even in the latter case, weaknesses emerged as a result of the informal nature of the conduct of the planning activity itself. Thus the three executive directors of the company, who form the planning team, maintain contact with the market through direct personal relationships, and do not consult the marketing department until an outline plan is drafted. The result is a tendency for all product-planning activities, from the search for product ideas

B

to commercialisation, to be dominated by the technical department. Clearly, unless the technical department has a mechanism whereby it can monitor and measure the nature of consumer or user demand, there is considerable potential for a mis-match between the technical department's conception of consumer needs and their reality. Such a mismatch must be regarded as a major cause of new product failures alluded to in the previous chapter.

SOME REASONS FOR LACK OF PRODUCT PLANNING

Smaller firms

In smaller firms, which generally implies relatively fewer product lines, the need for formal product-planning activities is less pressing. The interrelation of old and new products is well known to all those participating in planning, with the result that difficulties of co-ordination arise less frequently. There is less need for formal definitions of policies and objectives, whether corporate or product, because the smaller organisation is in a better position to disseminate management's thinking by informal means. A considerable doubt is, of course, that the management of the smaller firm in fact thinks in a clear way about its objectives. This may not always be the case, burdened as the management frequently is with short-term operating problems.

Technical orientation of management

In many firms, especially in the industrial market, the background and experience of managements are largely technical. Technically trained and orientated managers tend to be pre-occupied with the technical problems connected with their operations, with the result that their attitude to product planning is restricted to new-product development, particularly the technical or R and D phases. The result of this outlook is that the product-planning activity is incomplete. A striking example of this preoccupation with technical excellence is to be found in the case study describing the early development of the Solartron company in the United Kingdom.[5] Under the direction of John Bolton this company was a paradise for technical experts in the electronics field. Unfortunately, while the technical management were able to develop their ideas to the point where they were ready to be introduced into the market-place, manufacturing and sales were largely neglected. Accordingly, while investors were prepared to advance money on the technical potential of the company it was doing very little to generate cash inflow through the sale of its products. Ultimately the company was taken over as a ready-made R and D department of another company more sensitive to the need to translate technically sophisticated ideas into product sales.

Larger firms

The explanation for lack of product planning in larger, technically orientated firms appears to lie in a combination of the rapid growth that gave them large size, and the reasons already suggested above. Frequently these firms begin with technically orientated entrepreneurs whose business began round a single idea.[6] As the firm grows, the entrepreneurs become preoccupied with the problems of management while retaining a basic sympathy with the company's technical problems. The R and D effort, which was responsible for the birth and growth of the firm, becomes a dominant area of power. It is only later that other functions arise, and marketing is frequently the last of these functions to come into being. New-product development and maintenance of the product line are responsibilities borne by R and D, where most attention is paid to problems of technical development. The commercial side of the product line tends to be neglected. Even where product-maintenance responsibilities are given to the marketing function, as, for example, to a product manager, the working relationship between R and D and marketing is frequently not close.

As long as there is a lack of competition, and technical superiority is maintained, the pressures for more detailed, formal approaches to product planning are minimised. With the onset of greater competition the erosion of technological leads, and growing strain on informal methods as the company grows larger, the way is paved for the introduction of more formal product planning.

PRODUCT PLANNING – SOME TENTATIVE GENERALISATIONS

In later chapters in this book, we deal specifically with managerial approaches to product planning (Chapter 5) and various aspects of the planning process in relation to new-product development. As background to this more detailed analysis it will be useful at this time to try and state a few basic generalisations concerning product planning.

Empirical studies tend to suggest incomplete integration of product policies and objectives, new-product development, and maintenance of established product lines. Product planning and product development often concentrate only on the technical phrases of the new-product development process and pay inadequate attention to problems of discontinuing or modifying unprofitable or obsolete products. Further, concentration on technical aspects of product planning tend to result in neglect of the formulation of modified strategies for marketing an ever-changing range of products.

Some reasons which would seem to account for this imbalance in emphasis would seem to be:

(1) the importance of new-product development in terms of time, cost and historical contribution;

(2) technically orientated management; and

(3) reliance on informal methods appropriate to small firms which have not kept pace with the growth of company size.

Failure to integrate all phases of product planning and product development lead to a number of dangers. Among these may be cited the following:

(1) a firm may discover that it is selling a large volume of unprofitable products with no profitable new-product replacements potentially available;

(2) inadequate attention to product objectives and policies

may lead the firm in directions in which it had not intended to proceed;

(3) reliance on R and D may result in the initiating of too many development projects with the result that effort is dissipated over a wide area rather than concentrated on those with good commercial prospects.

These and other dangers which can weaken future growth argue the case for a strong, complete and formalised product-planning effort. A complete programme which allows for likely changes in the competitive situation facing businesses, and in the structure of the industry and the markets in which they operate, should help to avoid many dangers and increase the likelihood of profitable growth. We return to this theme in considerable detail in succeeding chapters.

Suggestions for further reading

James R. Bright, *Research, Development and Technical Innovation* (Homewood, Ill.: Irwin, 1964).

Theodore Levitt, 'When Science Supplants Technology', *Harvard Business Review* (July–Aug 1963) pp. 14–26.

Lewis N. Goslin, *The Product Planning System* (Homewood, Ill.: Irwin, 1967).

Chapter 3

Marketing Strategy and Product Policy

INTRODUCTION

In the previous chapter we expressed the view that the function of top management is to specify the nature of the firm's business, to articulate objectives to be achieved, to formulate a strategy for the achievement of the stated objectives, and to lay down policies whereby a chosen strategy may be implemented. In this chapter we develop the theme further by considering the relationship between marketing strategy and product policy prior to a more detailed examination of the different product strategies which appear to be open to a firm.

Although we have used the terms 'strategy' and 'policy' in the preceding paragraph in a manner which suggests that policy is subordinate to strategy, it must be stressed that the terms are frequently used as if they were interchangeable or, alternatively, as if strategy were subordinate to policy. While a number of fine distinctions have been made by a number of authors as to the true connotation of strategy and policy,[1] we do not consider that such distinctions are important to our purpose here. In the context of this book, strategy will be used in the sense of the means of achieving a stated objective. In the marketing context, strategy will specify the market objectives to be achieved as well as the marketing-mix appropriate to its achievements.

In the words of its originator, Neil Borden,[2] 'The marketing mix refers to the aportionment of effort, the combination, the designing, and the integration of the elements of marketing into a programme or "mix" which, on the basis of an appraisal of the market forces, will best achieve the objectives of an enterprise at a given time.' These mix elements include marketing research, product development, pricing, packaging, distribution, advertising and sales promotion, selling and merchandising, and after-sales service, and it is clear that the range of permutations and combinations of these elements is nearly infinite. Thus the role of the marketing strategist or planner is to develop specific policies for each of the mix elements in order to maximise their contribution to the achievement of the over-all objective.

Although we have stated that there is an almost infinite number of combinations of the mix elements, we also believe that fundamentally the firm has very few alternative strategies open to it, a view which we have expressed elsewhere under the rather grandiose title, 'The Concept of Limited Strategic Alternatives'.[3]

THE CONCEPT OF LIMITED STRATEGIC ALTERNATIVES

It is generally recognised that concepts of business strategy owe much to military thinking. It is fitting therefore that we develop our concept by reference to a simple military situation.

Like junior managers, junior military commanders are rarely if ever responsible for strategic decisions. However, the basic military problem is much the same at all levels of command, and it will be simpler to identify the alternative courses of action open at the sub-unit level rather than at the army level. Just as in a business context one is concerned with securing control over a market so, in the military sphere, one is concerned with exercising control over ground. Further, in order to encourage a positive frame of mind, early instruction in military tactics emphasises positive or attacking courses of action.

In the initial stages of their training junior military commanders are usually faced with a problem in which they are required to advance to a specified objective overcoming any resistance or obstacles placed in their way by the enemy. As is apparent from the simple diagram in Figure 3.1, only three choices are available – straight ahead, left flanking, or right flanking. At this level of training sub-unit commanders are not encouraged to think of other alternatives which may exist, and simplified assumptions are usually invoked, such that there is a preferred method of approach to the objectives which will become apparent after a proper appreciation of the problem.

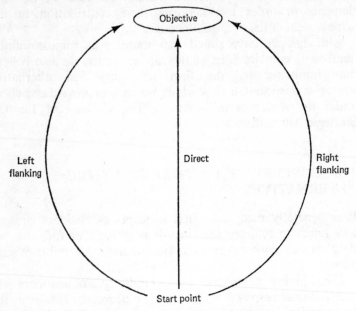

FIG. 3.1 *The 'attack' alternatives*

Further, on reaching the objective it is assumed that the attacker will find that he possesses the necessary superiority of force to overcome resistance.

Once familiarity has been gained with the basic problems then the assumptions can be relaxed. The first variation usually is that the attacker finds he has insufficient resources to overcome the enemy and so must be content to hold his own ground until such time as reinforcements can be brought forward and achieve the necessary superiority for the advance to continue. At even more sophisticated levels two further alternatives are recognised. The first is that the confrontation may be so unprofitable that the attacker will decide to withdraw from the conflict or, worse still, be subjected to a counter-attack by the enemy and forced to retreat.

The final alternative which may exist is one of bypassing the enemy. In military terms the use of airborne forces or the *blitzkreig* may be cited as examples of such a bypass strategy.

It is not difficult to draw a parallel between the simplified options available to the military commander and those which face firms competing in the market-place. A direct or head-on attack is normally only likely to succeed where the attacker possesses such a superiority of material that he can afford to squander his own resources in destroying a competitor. In business terms a head-on attack may be likened to the economist's concept of price competition between undifferen-tiated products, and be distinguished as a strategy of attrition. By contrast to direct or price competition many firms prefer to compete indirectly by pursuing a strategy of product dif-ferentiation, which in terms of our military analysis may be likened to a flanking attack.

The holding or do-nothing strategy is readily observed in many market situations and is claimed to be typical of oligopolistic conditions.

In the short term, withdrawal is a negative strategy. In the long term, it may enable the organisation, military or other-wise, to gather strength for a renewed attack or, alternatively, to change direction in pursuit of an alternative objective.

Finally, there is the bypass strategy which is almost invari-ably based upon innovation and is the strategy most likely to lead to a conclusive outcome. In the First World War, the de-velopment of the tank represented such an innovation and it might well have broken the stalemate of trench warfare had its existence not been revealed too soon. In the Second World War we have already referred to the impact of airborne forces and the concept of the *blitzkreig* to which must be added the ultimate innovation – the atomic bomb. In effect, the radical innovation changes the rules of the game and bestows an enormous superiority upon the innovator. It is for this reason that business firms concentrate so much effort upon R and D for, while most innovations will be relatively minor and lead only to a differentiated version of an existing product, there is always the possibility of achieving a breakthrough which will endow the innovator with a monopoly of the market, for example, the float-glass process, xerography and the Polaroid camera.

The existence of a limited range of basic strategies has also been commented on by Uyterhoeven,[4] whose list is similar to our own and recognises the following:

(1) the 'do-nothing' alternative;
(2) the liquidation alternative;
(3) the alternative of specialisation (concentrated marketing);
(4) the vertical-integration alternative;
(5) the diversification alternative; and
(6) the international alternative.

Similarly, Boggis[5] has suggested that the initiatives and responses open to the product strategist consist of six basic options:

(1) innovate;
(2) imitate – the 'fast-second', 'me-too', reverse-engineered solution;
(3) adopt – apply for a licence to manufacture;
(4) adapt – find a fresh application (will require (2) and (3) too);
(5) ignore – continue with existing product-mix; and
(6) resign – withdraw from this market, alter product-mix.

SELECTING A MARKETING STRATEGY

Of course, selection of a given basic strategy will depend upon a firm's perception of its own strengths and weaknesses *vis-à-vis* those of its competitors, and much will depend upon its relative standing in its existing markets. Although at first sight it appears that large firms have the greatest freedom of manoeuvre, such freedom is inevitably proscribed. The activities of large firms are likely to be much better known and documented than are those of their smaller rivals, especially in circumstances where their share of the market exceeds the arbitrary minimum which constitutes a legal monopoly, and this makes any change of direction conspicuous and the subject of comment. Further, very large companies are often expected to display greater social awareness and responsibility, and this too can circumscribe their scope for change, added to which the sheer inertia of the large corporation often militates against new initiatives.

While smaller firms would doubtless be glad to share some of the large firm's inertia in exchange for some of the security which size confers, their success generally depends upon their adopting a more opportunistic approach – an opportunism which Katz[6] has likened to guerilla warfare. Thus he comments: 'Essentially, the guerilla works on a relatively short time horizon, tries to maintain the initiative, and counts on his superior knowledge of the terrain (market) and populace (customers) to enable him to respond more quickly, more creatively, and more effectively than his larger and better financed opponent.' Katz continues to cite rules to govern such a guerilla strategy among which may be distinguished:

(1) attack when the enemy retreats, that is fill the niches left vacant by your competitor;

(2) do not take full advantage of all opportunities, that is retain some resources in reserve so you can deploy them quietly once it become clear where the best opportunities are;

(3) be as inconspicuous as possible, that is do not invite the attention of larger competitor;

(4) respond quickly, that is capitalise on ability to move before the slower and more cumbersome rival;

(5) retreat when the enemy attacks, that is do not court disaster by getting involved in a head-on clash.

Ideally, selection of a marketing strategy should be based upon the identification of a marketing opportunity which enables the firm to deploy its resource mix in the most profitable manner. We examine some approaches to the identification and measurement of market opportunity in the next chapter but at this juncture it will be useful to develop our present theme a little further by considering the basic marketing strategies open to a company.

Kotler[7] identifies three basic marketing strategies – undifferentiated marketing, differentiated marketing, and concentrated marketing. In his words

> Undifferentiated marketing exists where a firm chooses not to recognise the different demand curves that make up the market. Instead, it treats the market as an aggregate, focussing on what is common in the needs of people rather than on what is different. It tries to design a product and a marketing programme that appeals to the broadest number of buyers. It relies on mass channels, mass advertising media, and universal themes. It aims to endow the product with a superior image in people's minds, whether or not this is based on any real difference.

By contrast, 'under differentiated marketing, a firm decides to operate on all sides of the market but designs separate products and/or marketing programmes for each'. As Kotler notes, both differentiated and undifferentiated marketing imply that the firm is seeking to cover the whole market. For firms which feel that they have not the resources for such an all-embracing approach, concentrated marketing is based upon the selection of one or a limited number of segments within the market in which the firm will attempt to establish a dominant position. Which of these three strategies a firm should pursue depends, *inter alia*, upon its own resources, upon the nature and degree of competition in the market, and the degree of product and market homogeneity.

MARKET SEGMENTATION

In Chapter 1 we advanced the proposition that the opportunity to market differentiated products and services arises from the fact that, to some degree, all consumers or users differ from each other. Further, in the preceding section we have suggested that the choice of a basic marketing strategy is dictated by the degree to which sellers are prepared to recognise and cultivate such differences in demand by subdividing or segmenting it into smaller elements. It would seem appropriate therefore to devote some time to viewing the nature and applications of the concept of market segmentation.

While the concept of market segmentation has long been familiar to managers, it would seem that it was first articulated in its present form by Wendell R. Smith in 1956.[8] In this article, Smith draws the following differences between strategies of differentiation and segmentation:

In its simplest terms, *product differentiation* is concerned with the bending of demand to the will of supply. It is an attempt to shift or to change the slope of the demand curve for the market offering of an individual supplier. This strategy may also be employed by a group of suppliers such as a farm cooperative, the members of which have agreed to act together. It results from the desire to establish a kind of equilibrium in the market by bringing about adjustment of market demand to supply conditions favourable to the seller. . . . *Segmentation* is based upon developments on the demand side of the market and represents a rational and more precise adjustment of product and marketing effort to consumer or user requirements. In the language of the economist, segmentation is *disaggregative* in its effects and tends to bring about recognition of several demand schedules where only one was recognised before.

Thus the basic difference is between selling what you can make (differentiation) and making what you can sell (segmentation).

In so far as the distinction reflects the state of mind of the producer in his approach to the market it is useful in discriminating between a production orientation and a marketing orientation. However, while it is important that one should be sensitive to the theoretical implications of such discrimination it would be unwise to pursue it too far in practice. Taking the extreme case, a producer might acknowledge that the precise demand for all potential users of a particular product varies in some degree. On the other hand, the limitations imposed by his existing collection of physical resources and human skills might preclude the production of a large number of possible variants, while the economics of the manufacturing process would prevent the achievement of an acceptable market price for the desired degree of product variation. Such a producer could take the view that, owing to his inability precisely to satisfy demand, he should not produce at all. One is entitled to enquire if such rigid adherence to the extremist version of the marketing concept does not reduce consumer satisfaction below the level which would be attained had the same producer manufactured a standardised product incorporating the essential feature(s), (for example it washes clothes, is desired by potential customers), and then 'bent the will of demand to his supply'.

For this reason it is not recommended that one should dwell upon the subtle distinctions between differentiation and segmentation. In essence, the basic purpose is the same and stems from the same fundamental proposition that 'consumers are different'. Clearly, therefore, the important questions for the strategist are:

(1) Can we measure the differences between consumers?

(2) If yes, what methods are available, and what merits and demerits do these methods possess?

(3) What benefits can we anticipate from segmenting a market?

(4) What disadvantages are associated with segmenting a market?

We examine these questions in turn.

MEASURING CONSUMER DIFFERENCES

Superficially, concepts of market segmentation appear to have their widest application in the markets for consumer goods – certainly, judging by the published literature, much more research has been undertaken in this field than in the markets for industrial goods: in practice it seems likely that segmentation is used more extensively in industrial markets and that the technique has been used, albeit intuitively, for much longer. The reason why this should be so is not hard to find – it is more likely that the individual demand of a firm is of sufficient size to warrant the creation of a specific supply than is the demand of an individual person.

However, while it is readily acknowledged that there are marked differences of degree between consumer and industrial marketing, it is felt that in principle they are sufficiently alike to justify joint treatment: it will be obvious which techniques are unsuited or inappropriate to which type of market situation.

As Engel *et al*[9] have shown '. . . there are two ways to isolate segments within a market environment characterised by consumer dependent differences – (1) analysis of consumer characteristics (attribute differences) and (2) analysis of consumer response (behavioural differences)'. In essence, both techniques approach the same problem from different ends of the spectrum. Hence

> When one attempts to segment the market by the *analysis of attribute differences,* the usual procedure is to measure a number of consumer characteristics, such as personality, attitudes, age, income, social class, position in the family life-cycle and so on. Then determination is made of the extent to which variations in these characteristics relate to (and are thereby assumed to predict) variations in market behaviour (that is brand use, shopping patterns, media selections and so on). A different approach is the *analysis of behavioural differences.* The investigator begins with observed variations in behaviour or stated preferences (the end point in the above approach) and works backwards to variations in consumer attributes within the segments which result.[10]

Whichever method the analyst prefers, there is no shortage of variables which may prove useful discriminators. Conventionally these may be grouped into different categories and Kotler[11] proposes the following: demographic, geographic, buyer behaviour, and psychographic. Engel *et al*. suggest, on the other hand: socio-economic and demographic, geographic, psychological, product usage, perceptual, and brand loyalty. Both sources should be consulted for a detailed statement of the precise variables included in each category.

From the above quotations it is clear that Engel *et al*. are primarily interested in consumer markets. However, this emphasis upon individual characteristics is equally important in our view in helping distinguish the buying behaviour of different organisations. Firms, like people, possess demographics and factors such as size, the Standard Industrial Classification (S.I.C.) category, geographic location, and so on are all used in helping to segment industrial markets. Such criteria are relatively easy to identify and measure, and thus help to produce a broad market segmentation. However, if the industrial marketer wishes to refine his analysis and achieve a more precise segmentation then he must turn to a more detailed analysis of behavioural buying influences – both individual and group – in just the same manner as his consumer counterpart.[12]

In general, it is fair to say that demographics are fairly well-documented and accessible to the researcher. The same is rarely, if ever, true of behavioural data, although information on brand preferences and product usage is available for the more important consumer products in the publications of Neilsen and Attwood who monitor such markets on a continuous basis. In the absence of published data the analyst must collect his own, and we touch briefly on the available methods in the next chapter. As a generalisation, it seems to us that researchers tend to favour composite measures such as the well-known socio-economic categories (A, B, C1 etc.), or, more recently, the life-style approach popularised by Simon Broadbent. It also seems that the most successful segmentation strategy is likely to be the most sophisticated, in the sense of analysing large and complex data bases through techniques such as factor and cluster analysis, that is the fewer and simpler the factors used to differentiate a segment the more obvious it will be and the less likely that one can dominate such a segment with a truly distinctive product.

Engel *et al.* suggest three basic criteria for assessing the practical value of a market segment – its size, its 'reachability', and what we term its 'distinctiveness'. Size is an obvious criterion for judging whether or not a given market segment is worth exploiting although, clearly, it must be evaluated in light of the other two basic criteria which will affect the cost of reaching the segment and of competing for it. In terms of 'reaching' a market segment we have in mind the availability of media, through which differentiated communications may be directed at potential customers (Engel's interpretation), and also distribution channels. Distinctiveness is virtually self-explanatory and is a measure of the degree to which the behaviour of members of the chosen segment is different from the behaviour of other segments. Collectively the three criteria help establish whether and to what degree it is worth developing a product variant specifically for segment members as well as serving to cross-check that the segment is accessible and sufficiently well-defined/understood to represent a market opportunity.

This understanding of the nature of market opportunity is the major benefit of segmentation. From what has been said it is clear that the more detailed the analysis the more likely it is that one will discern a worthwhile market segment and the better fitted one will be to exploit it. Thus the firm which appreciates the value of such detailed information will seek to ensure that it acquires relevant data on a continuous basis. Further, by virtue of collecting such intelligence it will become sensitive to the degree and nature of competition in the various market segments and gain early warning of changes which may be taking place due to both internal and external forces. Founded on such an understanding a firm is in the best possible situation to identify realistic objectives for its own achievement and to plan ways and means of attaining them. In many instances the product will be selected as the appropriate medium and we turn now to consider basic product policies.

BASIC PRODUCT POLICIES

Other than in textbooks it rarely happens that an individual or group of people with access to capital will sit down to decide upon the production of a good or service for sale at a profit. More usually one is concerned with an on-going business with a given collection of skills and resources, some of them highly specific, and with a given product-mix. Accordingly it will be more realistic if we consider the second situation and identify the courses of action open to the firm.

Simplistically, the basic choice is whether to change the

TABLE 3.1 *Classification of new products by product objective*

PRODUCT OBJECTIVES	INCREASING TECHNOLOGICAL NEWNESS		
	NO TECHNOLOGICAL CHANGE	IMPROVED TECHNOLOGY To utilise more fully the company's present scientific knowledge and production skills.	NEW TECHNOLOGY To acquire scientific knowledge and production skills new to the company.
NO MARKET CHANGE		*Reformulation* To maintain an optimum balance of cost, quality, and availability in the formulas of present company products. Example: use of oxidised microcrystaline waxes in Glo-Coat (1946).	*Replacement* To seek new and better ingredients or formulation for present company products in technology not now employed by the company. Example: development of synthetic resin as a replacement for shellac in Glo-Coat (1950).
STRENGTHENED MARKET To exploit more fully the existing markets for the present company products.	*Remerchandising* To increase sales to consumers of types now served by the company. Example: use of dripless spout can for emulsion waxes (1955).	*Improved product* To improve present products for greater utility and merchandisability to consumers. Example: combination of auto paste wax and cleaner into one-step 'J-Wax' (1956).	*Product-line extension* To broaden the line of products offered to present consumers through new technology. Example: development of a general purpose floor cleaner 'Emeral' in maintenance product line (1953).
NEW MARKET To increase the number of types served by the company.	*New use* To find new classes of consumers that can utilise present company products. Example: sale of paste wax to furniture manufacturers for Caul Board wax (1946).	*Market extension* To reach new classes of consumers by modifying present products. Example: wax-based coolants and drawing compounds for industrial machining operations (1951).	*Diversification* To add to the classes of consumers served by developing new technical knowledge. Example: development of 'Raid' – dual purpose insecticide (1955).

INCREASING MARKET NEWNESS

Source: Johnson and Jones, 'How to Organise New Products', *Harvard Business Review* (May–June 1957) p. 52.

product or not. If it is decided not to change the product, then the firm is committed to a strategy of undifferentiated marketing. Conversely, if it is prepared to entertain changes in the product itself, then it will pursue a strategy of differentiated marketing. If in both cases the firm's over-all objective is to increase sales and profitability, then a strategy of undifferentiated marketing demands that the market be extended, while a strategy of differentiated marketing offers the possibility of entering new and different markets.

An extremely useful way of considering the implications of these alternatives is presented in the matrix (Table 3.1), which is taken from an approach first advanced by Samuel C. Johnson and Conrad Jones.[13] As this matrix makes it clear, the company has four basic choices open to it:

(1) it can pursue a no-change strategy;

(2) it can pursue a strategy of undifferentiated marketing but seek to strengthen its position through increasing brand preference (remerchandising) or market development (new use);

(3) it can pursue a strategy of differentiated marketing on a limited scale by offering improved products into its existing market (reformulation and replacement); and

(4) it can pursue a policy of differentiated marketing on an ambitious scale by changing both the product and the marketing approach simultaneously.

Three of these alternatives – improved product, product-line extension, and market extension still retain contact with the firm's former business along one dimension. The fourth alternative – diversification – takes it into a completely new area.

While the first alternative – the no-change strategy – appears to be the least risky at first sight, it is clear that in a dynamic competitive environment, it is likely to prove the most risky strategy in the long run. Conversely, while diversification may seem the most risky alternative, in the long run it may offer the best opportunity for continued growth and profitability. Thomas Staudt cites six major reasons why companies diversify which he further subdivides into forty-three specific reasons.[14] These are:

A. *Survival*

(1) To offset declining or vanishing markets,
(2) To compensate for technological obsolescence,
(3) To offset obsolete facilities,
(4) To offset declining profit margins, and
(5) To offset an unfavourable geographic location brought about by changing economic factors.

B. *Stability*

(1) To eliminate or offset seasonal slumps,
(2) To offset cyclical fluctuations,
(3) To maintain employment of the labour force,
(4) To provide balance between high-margin and low-margin products,
(5) To provide balance between old and new products,
(6) To maintain market share,
(7) To meet new products of competitors,
(8) To tie customers to the firm,
(9) To distribute risk by serving several small markets,
(10) To maintain an assured source of supply.
(11) To assure an outlet from the sale of the product, and
(12) To develop a strong competitive supply position by offering several close substitute products.

C. *Productive utilisation of resources*

(1) To utilise waste or by-products,
(2) To maintain balance in vertical integration,
(3) To make use of basic raw materials,
(4) To utilise excess productive capacity,
(5) To make use of innovations from internal technical research,
(6) To capitalise distinctive knowhow,
(7) To make full use of management resources,
(8) To utilise excess marketing capacity,
(9) To exploit the value of an established market position, trade name, or prestige,
(10) To keep pace with an ever-increasing rate of technology,

(11) To capitalise on company research with existing techniques as well as its advances in technology, and
(12) To capitalise on a firm's market contacts.

D. *Adaptation to change in customer needs*

(1) To meet the demands or convenience of diversified dealers,
(2) To meet the specific requests of important individuals and/or groups of customers,
(3) To meet government requests for national security, and
(4) To improve performance of existing products (equipment) through adding accessories or complementary products.

E. *Growth*

(1) To counter market saturation on present products,
(2) To reinvest earnings,
(3) To take advantage of unusually attractive merger or acquisition opportunities,
(4) To stimulate the sale of basic products, and
(5) To encourage growth for its own sake or to satisfy the ambitions of management or owners.

F. *Miscellaneous*

(1) To realise maximum advantages from the tax structure,
(2) To salvage or make the best of previously acquired companies or products,
(3) To maintain reputation for industrial leadership,
(4) To comply with the desires (or whims) of owners or executives, and
(5) To strengthen the firm by obtaining new management and abilities.

Probably the easiest route to diversification is through merger or acquisition. Certainly this was the method preferred by the conglomerate organisations which sprang to such prominence during the 1960s. However, it would seem that much of the conglomerate's success was due to the revaluation of under-employed or under-valued assets. Once this 'profit' had been taken, the management of the conglomerate found itself in control of a heterogeneous group of companies lacking a common thread in terms of their technology or product base. In light of this deficiency most firms considering diversification now seek to do so from their own resource base or, alternatively, seek to acquire another organisation which complements their own on-going business.

SUMMARY

In this chapter we have suggested that marketing strategy sets out the general means whereby a company is to achieve its over-all objective. We have further suggested that there is only a small range of basic strategies which are open to the company but that product policy plays a central role in them all. Again, while there is a limited portfolio of product strategies, the basic purpose must be to select that which offers the company the best opportunity to use its resources profitably. It follows that the ability to measure market opportunity is fundamental to the selection of a product strategy and it is to this topic that we turn in the next chapter.

Suggestions for further reading

Kenneth R. Andrews, *The Concept of Corporate Strategy* (Homewood, Ill.: Irwin 1971).

H. Igor Ansoff, *Corporate Strategy* (Harmondsworth: Penguin, 1968).

Martin L. Bell, *Marketing Concepts and Strategy* (London: Macmillan, 1966).

Chapter 4

Identifying Market Opportunities

INTRODUCTION

A recurring theme of the preceding three chapters has been the need for a company to specify the objective or objectives which it wishes to achieve, and, through the formulation of a strategy, the means by which this is to be achieved. We have also stressed the central role played by the product or service as the medium through which corporate strategy is implemented. Thus, of all the policies relating to the various elements of the marketing-mix, product policy invariably takes pride of place, for, whereas a given product policy does not predetermine policies regarding packaging, distribution, promotion and selling activity, and so forth, it does have a very important influence upon them, and more often than not must be determined prior to considering these other policies.

While recognising that the textbook approach to marketing with its emphasis upon pre-identification of market opportunity as a basis for the formulation of strategy is a counsel of perfection and of limited immediate utility to the firm with an existing product-mix, it seems clear that the long-run survival of all organisations is highly dependent upon their ability both to forecast the nature of change in the future and also to respond to it. It also seems clear that if marketing research is to be effective as an input into marketing planning, then it must be undertaken on a continuous basis. In this chapter we briefly consider methods of identifying and measuring market opportunity.

THE NATURE OF MARKETING OPPORTUNITY

In a well-known work[1] Martin L. Bell defines a marketing opportunity as 'a challenge to purposeful marketing action, that is characterised by a generally favourable set of environmental circumstances and an acceptable probability of success'. Certain important points are implicit in this definition. First is the point that marketing opportunities arise from a favourable combination of circumstances in the environment in which the company is operating (or wishes to operate in) in accordance with its declared objectives. Thus a generally favourable set of environmental conditions only represents a marketing opportunity when it enables a particular organisation to deploy its resources more effectively than it could in any alternative investment opportunity open to it. The second point implicit in the definition is that marketing opportunities enjoy an existence independent of the firm and may only be realised by purposeful action on the part of the firm. Finally, the definition makes it clear that marketing opportunities can only have a probability of success – rarely, if ever, is an opportunity such that success can be guaranteed.

Bell continues to describe the fundamental marketing opportunity as the chance to provide satisfactions. As we saw in Chapter 1, it is satisfactions that consumers wish to acquire, and the range and extent of these are virtually limitless. However, the provision of satisfactions is the basic purpose of all marketing and as a statement is of little practical use as a basis for planned action. Accordingly Bell suggests that marketing opportunities fall into four basic categories: the opportunity to innovate; the opportunity to improve efficiency; the opportunity to create a competitive difference; and the opportunity to carve out a market niche. In this context Bell is using 'innovate' in the widest sense to include not only product innovation but also innovation in the means of distributing and promoting products. This is a highly positive approach to marketing and what may be termed a 'leading' strategy.[2]

However, all companies do not wish to be leaders and a number of very successful companies have preferred to adopt a following strategy. Such a strategy is implicit in Bell's 'opportunity to improve efficiency'. As is apparent in the statistics of new-product failures, innovation is a risky business and many companies prefer to take a wait-and-see posture, relying on their ability to improve upon either the product or its marketing when they see a new product which appears to be gaining acceptance with users and consumers. Levitt has characterised this approach as 'imitative innovation'.[3]

In the context in which we have described them the opportunity to innovate and to improve efficiency largely corresponds to our strategy of undifferentiated marketing discussed in the previous chapter. Similarly, the opportunity to create a competitive difference is the same as differentiated marketing, and the opportunity to carve out a market niche conforms with our description of concentrated marketing.

However, regardless of the manner in which we choose to categorise marketing opportunities they can only be relevant if they are first identified.

IDENTIFYING MARKETING OPPORTUNITIES

The search for and acquisition of data has been defined by Aguilar[4] as falling into four categories:

(1) undirected viewing,
(2) conditioned viewing,
(3) informal search, and
(4) formal search.

'Undirected viewing is defined as general exposure to information where the viewer has no specific purpose in mind, with the possible exception of exploration.' Conversely, 'conditioned viewing is defined as directed exposure not involving active search, to a more or less clearly identified area or to a type of information' – in other words, the viewer is conscious of a generalised need for particular types of information and so is likely to recognise relevant data. As the name suggests, informal search implies that one is actively seeking information for a particular purpose but in an unstructured manner, while 'formal search refers to a deliberate effort – usually following a pre-established plan, procedure or methodology –

to secure specific information, or information related to a specific issue'.

It is clear that market opportunity may be identified as a result of any of these types of scanning the environment, but it is also clear that in order to evaluate properly the nature of any given opportunity one must ultimately subject it to a formal search procedure. Thus Aguilar's model suggests a hierarchy in which one moves from a vague and generalised awareness to conscious awareness, interest, and active and formalised search. In the nature of things, the severer the competitive pressures which a company is experiencing the more short term and focused is likely to be its search for marketing opportunities.

It is widely accepted that while long-range planning cannot completely eliminate the need for short-term reactions to competitive threats, none the less the company which invests some of its resources in attempting to predict the nature of the future environment is less likely to be caught out than the company which lives solely in the short term. Obviously the further ahead one looks the less certain one can be about the accuracy of one's predictions. On the other hand, it is clear that if the firm is unable to make a generalised statement as to where it wishes to be at some future point in time, it is not in a very good position to develop a plan for getting from where it currently is to where it wants to be. For this reason there has been considerable growth of interest in long-range planning in recent years, accompanied by a significant improvement in the range and sophistication of the techniques available to the long-range planner. Some of the better known of these approaches are described below.

THE DELPHI MODEL

In essence the Delphi approach to technological forecasting represents a structured approach to the intuitive thinking or brain-storming processes familiar to most executives who have been called upon to make a long-range forecast. The technique itself was developed mainly by Olaf Helmer at the RAND Corporation and seeks to achieve a consensus of expert opinion as the result of a series of rounds of individual forecasts.

By contrast with brain-storming procedures where the experts interact with one another on a face-to-face basis, participants in a Delphi forecast rarely if ever meet, and frequently are not informed of the identity of other experts contributing to the exercise. The first phase of constructing a Delphi forecast usually consists of asking each expert to submit their individual opinion concerning the likelihood of some future event. For example, experts on transportation might be asked to project the types of transportation system which might be in use between the years 2000 and 2025. The initial responses would be analysed and the second round of consultation would probably consist of asking the experts to attach their own estimates of the relative importance of the most frequently mentioned forms of transportation as a basis for rank ordering in terms of importance. Depending upon the precise needs of the forecaster the experts may then be asked to express opinions on specific transportation options given the consensus of importance attached to each of them.

Although the Delphi method seeks to achieve a consensus among a group of experts, it does so in a more objective manner than would be possible where the personalities of the participants were allowed to interact with one another. The method has been used fairly extensively, particularly in forecasting developments in weapons systems and space programmes, and is claimed to be of most use in formulating goals for long-range achievement.

SCENARIO WRITING

Probably the best example of scenario writing is to be found in a book written by Herman Kahn and Anthony J. Wiener.[5] This book arose out of the joint interest of the American Academy of Arts and Sciences and the Hudson Institute in attempting to set down the nature of 'alternative futures'. In developing their 'framework for speculation', the team used 'several inter-related devices to facilitate making systematic conjectures about the future. The most important, of course, is simply to think about the problem – to seek to identify important long-term trends which seem likely to continue.' The team found that there are basic long-term multiple trends toward

(1) increasingly sensate (empirical, this worldly, secular, humanistic, pragmatic, utilitarian, contractual, epicurean, or hedonistic, and the like) cultures;

(2) bourgeois bureaucratic, 'meritocratic', democratic (and nationalistic?) elites;

(3) accumulation of scientific and technological knowledge;

(4) institutionalisation of change, especially research, development, innovation and diffusion;

(5) world-wide industrialisation and modernisation;

(6) increasing affluence and (recently) leisure;

(7) population growth;

(8) urbanisation and (soon) the growth of megalopolises;

(9) decreasing importance of primary and (recently) secondary occupations;

(10) literacy and education;

(11) increasing incapability for mass destruction;

(12) increasing tempo of change; and

(13) increasing universality of the multifold trend.

Based upon the identification of these basic trends, the team then proceed to consider their implications for society under various assumptions of the most likely future events. As Jantsch[6] has pointed out, the primary purpose is not to predict the future but systematically to explore branching points depending upon critical choices.

It is clear that both the Delphi and scenario techniques as developed at the Hudson Institute represent a more structured and formalised approach to other more familiar opinion-based methods such as the committee and brain-storming approaches.

EXTRAPOLATIVE TECHNIQUES

Within this category are included a whole battery of methods which extrapolate forward from currently available data. In

Jantsch's opinion, straight predictions may only be ventured for periods up to about fifteen years, which is identified as the average time span between a scientific discovery and technological innovation. Beyond this, time-span forecasting becomes much more speculative. One of the dangers is that by projecting forward currently identifiable trends, one may give a spurious impression of accuracy in one's forecast. Such a risk is noticeable in the forecasts contained in *Limits to Growth* by Meadows *et al.* in which exponential functions are used to show that, given the projected growth in population and continued increases in consumption, many vital resources will be exhausted early in the second millennium. Past experience would tend to suggest that there are potentially a very large number of developments which could totally change the pessimistic nature of these projections, for example most economic growth in the past century has arisen from improved technology rather than from increases in factor inputs.

STRUCTURING METHODS

The major techniques to be found in this category are morphological research, normative relevance tree techniques, and systems analysis. All these techniques possess the common feature that, in the words of the pioneer of morphological research, Fritz Zwickey, they constitute 'an orderly way of looking at things'.[8]

The approach followed in morphological research is to reduce problems to their basic parameters and then consider the various combinations and permutations of these basic parameters. Jantsch cites as an example the case of a simple chemical jet engine which is characterised by eleven basic parameters that can be so combined as to give 25,344 different solutions. Among these possible solutions several are likely to be highly novel and unlikely to have been conceived of without considering all the possible alternatives stipulated as a result of the morphological research.

The normative relevance tree approach attacks the forecasting problem from the other end, in that it states first the goals and objectives of the organisation and then examines the alternatives open for the possible achievement of these objectives. Analogously the goals and objectives comprise the trunk and the alternatives the branches. By progressing along the alternatives or branches, the analysis becomes progressively more intensive and results in a statement of deficiency in the existing state of science and technology. Normative relevance tree techniques were widely used in the NASA Apollo programme.

Systems analysis *per se* is probably a more familiar approach to the statement of problems than either of the structuring methods described above. This familiarity owes much to the spread of operational research techniques and to the development of the electronic computer, both of which rest heavily upon systems analysis.

The value of technological forecasting is eloquently summarised by Olaf Helmer[9] when he comments that

a fatalistic view that the future is unforeseeable and inevitable is being abandoned. It is being recognised that there are a multitude of possible futures and that appropriate intervention can make a difference to their probabilities. This raises the exploration of the future, and the search for ways to influence this direction, to activities of great social responsibility.

However, as noted when discussing the Delphi method, most technological forecasts are of greatest value in formulating objectives which set out where the organisation hopes to be at some future time. Based upon the statement of such long-term objectives the function of the long-range planner is to specify how the organisation is to get from where it is to where it wants to be, and for setting out the checkpoints through which it will be necessary to pass in order to attain the desired goal. Ideally the company should have a very clear picture of its current standing, of the acceptability of its product-mix and the success which it is enjoying in the market-place, and of its strengths and weaknesses *vis-à-vis* its competition. In practice, only a very small proportion of all companies have made a formal inventory of their resources, which is up-dated in the light of new experience. It follows, therefore, that in determining which of a number of possible future courses of action are open to it, the firm must first undertake a thorough audit of its current status.

AUDITING THE COMPANY'S STATUS

An audit of an organisation's status falls naturally into two parts – an internal and an external audit.

The subject of the internal management audit has been treated extensively by a number of authors. In the area of product strategy, it would be difficult to improve upon the readings selected by Berg and Shuchman in *Product Strategy and Management*.[10] Despite its age this volume is virtually a definitive source book on the subject of product management and much that has been written since leans on the original contributions contained in it. It would be duplicative, therefore, to repeat the content of Alexander, Cross and Cunningham's treatment of the appraisal of company strengths and weaknesses, Philip Marvin's article on 'Auditing Product Programmes' or D'Orsey Hurst's 'Criteria for Evaluating Existing Products and Product Lines'.[11] Bell, in his contribution, analysing the marketing situation, dwells at some length on a consideration of the marketing audit,[12] while an excellent checklist of the issues to be covered is contained in the *Marketing Handbook*.[13] Collectively there is a large measure of agreement between these writers that the audit should cover most, if not all, of the points listed below.[14]

Physical Resources: (a), *land* as a source of raw materials, and, as a location for manufacturing and distributive activities; (b) *buildings* – general purpose or specific, that is designed for light engineering, assembly, storage, and so forth, or for heavy manufacturing requiring special foundations, services, and so on; (c) *availability of and access to* power supplies, drainage and waste disposal, and to transportation – road, rail, canal, port facilities and the like; (d) *plant and equipment* – general purpose, for example lathes and presses, or, specific, for example steel-rolling mills, foundries and the like.

Technical Resources. Essentially these reside in the technical expertise of the firm's employees, together with the possession of patents, licences or highly specialised equipment.

Financial Resources. These are comprised of the liquid assets in the firm's balance sheet, the ability to secure loans against fixed assets, and the ability to raise capital in the market on the basis of past and anticipated future performance. They also comprise the skill of the firm's financial management.

Purchasing Resources. Managerial expertise backed by any special advantage enjoyed by the firm by virtue of its size or connections, for example reciprocal trading agreements.

Labour Resources. The skills, experience, and adaptability of the work force.

Marketing Resources. The degree of consumer/user acceptance or 'franchise' developed through past performance. Access to and degree of control over distribution; the specialised skills and experience of its personnel.

A similar measure of agreement also exists concerning the structure of an audit of the external environment and is well exemplified in Table 4.1.

Clearly, the conduct of an external audit will require the company to obtain and evaluate relevant information on a number of factors. We conclude this chapter with a brief review of the available sources of information and the means of obtaining them.

THE COLLECTION OF DATA

Where research is being initiated for the first time, or a specific *ad hoc* investigation is to be undertaken, data collection will only be embarked upon after a number of preliminary activities have been satisfactorily completed. Assuming that the firm has recognised the need for research, then the next step must be a precise statement of the problem to be investigated. Given an

TABLE 4.1   *Steps in auditing the competitive environment*

		Key elements

Step one: Define the market

Develop:
1. Statement of purpose in terms of user benefits
2. Product scope
3. Size, growth rate, maturity stage, need for primary versus selective strategies
4. Requirements for success
5. Divergent definitions of the above by competitors
6. Definition to be used by the company

Step two: Determine performance differentials

1. Evaluate industry performance and company difference
2. Determine differences in products, applications, geography, and distribution channels
3. Determine differences by customer set

Step three: Determine differences in competitive programmes

Identify and evaluate individual companies for their:
1. Market development strategies
2. Product development strategies
3. Financing and administrative strategies and support

Step four: Profile the strategies of competitors

1. Profile each significant competitor and/ or distinct type of composite strategy
2. Compare own and competitive strategies

Step five: Determine strategic planning structure

When size and complexity are adequate:
1. Establish planning units or cells and designate prime and subordinate dimensions
2. Make organisational assignments to product managers, industry managers, and others

---

Source: J. Thomas Cannon, *Business Strategy and Policy* (New York: Harcourt, Brace & World, 1968) p. 102.

C

agreed problem definition, it becomes possible to define precise objectives for any research which needs to be undertaken to make good deficiencies in existing information. Research objectives lay down what is to be investigated. The experimental or survey design states how this is to be done.

Invariably the structure of a research design recognises the existence of two main types of data – primary and secondary. While primary data must be gathered from original sources by the researcher, secondary data have already been collected, albeit for some other purpose, and so should be consulted first.

The investigation of secondary data, or desk research, should always begin with an examination of the company's own records and information system. Elsewhere,[15] it has been suggested that internal records will usually exist for the following:

(1) purchasing – stock levels, unit cost, usage rates, and so on;
(2) production – output, material, labour, inventory, physical distribution and overhead costs, machine utilisation, and so on;
(3) personnel – wage costs, turnover, efficiency levels, absenteeism, and so on;
(4) marketing – promotional and administrative expenditure, market and brand data, and so on;
(5) sales – by product volume, value, contribution to profit, order size, by type of outlet/customer, and by area and by salesmen; and
(6) finance – all cost and accounting data.

Once the firm has screened its own internal records, there are a large number of external sources of information which may possess data relevant to its needs. Such external sources may conveniently be grouped into five categories:

(1) government sources, both domestic and foreign;
(2) universities and research organisations, for example the Building Research Establishment and the National Engineering Laboratory;
(3) trade associations and chambers of commerce;
(4) publications – academic, professional, trade; and
(5) commercial research organisations and media owners, for

example the Economist Intelligence Unit, Gallup, Nielsen, the Financial Times, and so forth.

A useful summary of literature sources is reproduced in Table 4.2.

As we noted earlier, secondary data will usually have been

TABLE 4.2 *Literature sources*

A. *Technical Information*

Source	Information
Scientific, technical and engineering journals and conferences, Patents	Specialised technical data on performance characteristics, applications, process/ manufacturing control parameters
Professional Institution, Learned Society membership lists	Individual and corporate contacts in specific technological areas
Popular technical press, quality newspapers	General surveys on technologies and news of current technological and engineering events

B. *Commercial information*

Source	Information
Quality newspapers, N.E.D.O. reports, Government surveys, O.E.C.D., U.N., E.E.C., surveys	Specific industry surveys covering future needs and prospects
National and international statistics, census statistics, D.T.I. Business Monitor, Trade Association statistics	Statistical, economic and demographic data assisting in demand forecasts
Trade directories, yearbooks, Central Register of Businesses, general directories	Data on companies in potential industry markets
Company reports, financial press	Data on specific companies

C. *Location of information*

University, Research Association and other libraries, Patents Office, N.R.L.S.I.	Scientific, technical and engineering information, journal articles, conference and other papers
Research stations, Trade Associations	Specific industry technical, information and statistical data
Government Departments, Central Statistical Office, Business Statistics Office	Government statistics
Market Intelligence Library (D.T.I.)	Overseas and International Statistics
Register of Companies	Company information
Own Library	Collection of sources and material

collected for other purposes and may not be suitable to the researcher's needs. In any event, it is essential that all such data should be checked for impartiality, validity and reliability.

Only rarely will a company be fortunate enough to find all the information it needs in existing sources. To a greater or lesser degree the available information will be deficient in some way, and this deficiency will have to be remedied by original research to collect primary data.

FIELD RESEARCH

As Kotler points out,[16] primary data may be generated in four ways – observation, experimentation, interviewing and expert estimation. Of these four alternatives, observation and expert opinion are frequently used for developing hypotheses which may be tested by means of either experimentation or by interviewing a representative sample of respondents. The latter approach is the most familiar and most widely used of the four methods.

The design and execution of sample surveys is a subject in its own right, and a number of references are given at the end of this chapter for those seeking a full treatment. However, for our purposes it will suffice to indicate the basic steps involved in undertaking a survey and the interviewing alternatives which are available.

Although one will normally have consulted secondary sources and so have some understanding of the main dimensions of the problem to be investigated by means of a survey, it is usual to carry out a number of relatively informal preliminary interviews in order to determine how respondents talk and think about the subject of investigation. Based upon these preliminary interviews, it is normal to develop a pilot questionnaire for further testing. Concurrent with the questionnaire design, the researcher will have to decide the interviewing method to be used as well as the sample design to be followed.

In the majority of cases researchers wish to have some measure of the reliability of the data collected by means of a sample survey and so will use a probability-based sample design, for example random, stratified or multi-stage sampling. However, where statistical accuracy and/or predictive ability are of secondary importance, as is often the case in an attitude survey, then the researcher may choose to use a non-probability sample in which respondents are selected on the basis of convenience, judgement or some predetermined quota. Such non-probability-based sampling methods are much easier and cheaper to execute and frequently generate data as good as that which may be obtained from a probability-based sample.

Three methods of interviewing are open to the researcher: by personal, face-to-face interviews, by telephone, and by post. Personal interviewing is to be preferred where it is not ruled out by reasons of cost and/or time. It is the most flexible method and can handle questions of far greater complexity than is possible in the case of either a telephone or mail survey. Response rates are much higher than for the two other methods and it is probably the only viable way of satisfactorily completing a probability-based sample.

Telephone interviewing is widely used in the United States for both consumer and industrial surveys. However, in this country, there are far fewer personal telephone subscribers and these tend to be concentrated in the upper socio-economic groups. Accordingly the telephone is only appropriate for consumer surveys where respondents are to be drawn from these groups, but telephone interviewing is becoming increasingly popular in the execution of industrial surveys.

The mail survey can be used for collecting both industrial and consumer data but suffers from two major deficiencies. First, the respondent can read the whole questionnaire prior to answering any questions, and this may bias or condition his responses. Second, mail questionnaires lack the immediacy of personal or telephone interviewing methods and over-all response rates tend to be low.

In the final analysis the method of data collection and sample design are invariably determined on the basis of the time and cost involved. A useful aid to deciding just how much it is worth spending on data collection is to be found in the concept of the expected value of perfect information. This concept has been derived from statistical decision theory which has developed from the applications of Bayes theorem. However, in very simple terms, the expected value of perfect information is the difference between the outcome of an investment decision made under conditions of certainty and the outcome projected by the decision-maker who lacks such certain information and so must forecast an expected value based on his own best judgement.[17]

Suggestions for further reading

Joan McFarlane-Smith, *Interviewing in Market and Social Research*, (London: Routledge & Kegan Paul, 1972).

C. A. Moser and G. Kalton, *Survey Methods in Social Investigation*, 2nd edn (London: Heinemann, 1971).

A. N. Oppenheim, *Questionnaire Design and Attitude Measurement*, (London: Heinemann, 1967).

S. Payne, *The Art of Asking Questions* (Princeton University Press, 1951).

Chapter 5

Product Management

The foregoing chapter has emphasised the importance of existing skills and capabilities available to the firm – assessed through auditing – and has suggested technological forecasting as a means whereby an attempt can be made to gauge emerging market opportunities. Ideally, the end result of these activities should be the continuous and systematic adjustment of the firm's resources to its emerging environment through the link of the product it sells. This, however, raises the crucial issue of how these products are to be most effectively managed. It is to this problem we now turn, paying particular attention to the role of the product-manager system.

BASIC APPROACHES TO THE MANAGEMENT OF PRODUCTS

Before adopting a specific tactic, such as appointing a product manager, Mancuso[1] warns that it is wiser to be sure that the basic marketing strategy is sound in the first place. Once the strategy is established various tactical possibilities can be considered. Might it be more sensible to have market managers or sales managers? Mancuso gives three examples to show the possibilities open to the firm:

(1) where the company sells many products, though similar distribution channels, to the same customers, product managers are most applicable, for example in the case of electronic instrumentation;

(2) where a limited number of products (for example elastic bands) are sold to a wide number of industries through multiple channels, market managers may be a better choice;

(3) For a situation which falls somewhere between the two extremes (for example household paints) organisation around a sales manager may be entirely appropriate.

Ames,[2] too, dwells on the alternatives to product managers, and suggests three of these (see Figure 5.1):

(1) separate divisions for complete product specialisation;
(2) separate product marketing groups; and
(3) separate product sales forces.

Clearly no single approach is suitable to all organisations, and currently a debate revolves around the issue of product managers versus market managers. Before turning to look in detail at the product-manager system, it is intended first of all to say something about this controversy.

PRODUCT MANAGERS vs MARKET MANAGERS

Although there are differences of opinion as to the product manager's responsibility and authority, which are discussed below, his role is clearly defined as a co-ordinator of all activities related to the marketing of a specific product. By contrast, the role of the market manager is open to debate.

Theoretically, the position of market manager implies that an individual is appointed to co-ordinate all marketing activities appropriate to the needs of a specific market. The position is a staff appointment which may carry certain executive authority *vis-à-vis* other staff functions, but stands in contrast to the position of *marketing* manager which is a wholly executive function. Unfortunately the terms 'market manager' and 'marketing manager' are used loosely as if they were interchangeable. Hence the true role may only be determined by reference to the specific tasks performed. Neither product nor market managers have any direct authority over the field sales force whereas the marketing manager does. In addition, a marketing manager has both a line and staff responsibility and authority – in essence he is responsible not only for the preparation of the marketing plan but for its implementation, and so exercises control over the physical distribution function as well as field sales.

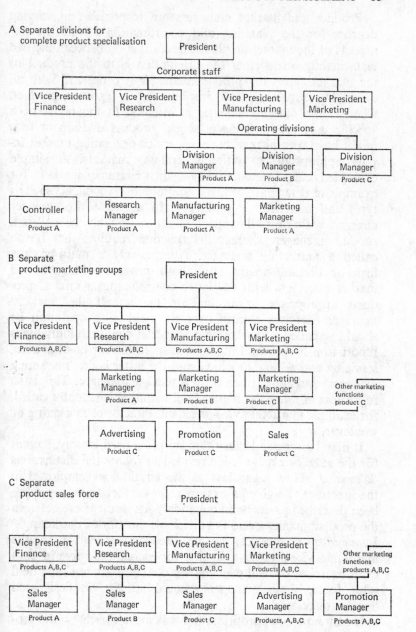

FIG. 5.1. *Basic approaches to product management*

Product and market managers are responsible in varying degrees for the planning and co-ordination of all 'service' aspects of the marketing plan. The distinction between the two rests mainly on whether the orientation is to the product or the market. Thus the product manager is concerned with all marketing aspects which impinge on a specific product, whereas the market manager is oriented to the needs of a specific user group. Thus a 'single' product division or firm might have several market managers co-ordinating market inputs appropriate to different end-use markets. A simple example is sales to industrial as against consumer markets, for example of detergent products, automobile components such as tyres and batteries, or stationery. In this case the manager charged with over-all control might reasonably be called a product manager whereas his function requires that he be called a marketing manager. Alternatively a multi-product firm or division might have both product managers and market managers with the latter co-ordinating a mix of products appropriate to an end-use market. If the 'market' manager exercises control over the field sales operation he should be called a 'marketing manager'. Often such individuals report to a higher-level manager responsible for co-ordinating servicing and selling, in which case the latter is the 'marketing manager' and the former truly a market manager. This is so regardless of what the higher-level manager is actually called, for example marketing vice-president, director of marketing or whatever.

It may be repeated that titles are often used loosely, so that for the sake of clarity it is intended to follow the distinctions delineated above regardless of the terminology employed in the literature. To give an example, the marketing manager has been described as one who commonly fits 'somewhere between the product manager and the division's director of marketing'.[3] In smaller companies, he is directly responsible to the marketing vice-president. In that the higher executive in both cases exercises control over the 'marketing managers' and field sales force, these managers should strictly be designated 'market managers'.

It may now be appropriate to focus more closely on the product-manager concept.

THE PRODUCT MANAGER

It is often implied that the product-manager concept is of recent origin, but there is evidence to suggest that General Electric had adopted such a title as early as 1894 while Libby McNeil and Libby claim 'to have had a primitive product manager program in 1919'.[4] Generally, however, the introduction of the concept is credited to one of its leading exponents, Proctor and Gamble, who appointed a brand manager for Lava soap in 1928.

The *raison d'être* of the product management system is that it ensures that 'sufficient individual attention (is devoted) to the planning, development and sale of each product in each market place'.[5]

Primarily the product manager's function is one of liaison between the various functional departments of the firm to ensure optimum co-ordination of their activities and hence maximise his particular product's contribution to over-all profitability. The interfaces with which the product manager must deal have been described by Luck as being perhaps the most numerous and varied of any middle manager.[6] This writer lists these interfaces as follows:

(1) the buying public;
(2) distributors;
(3) sales force;
(4) advertising agencies;
(5) purchasing officers;
(6) marketing research;
(7) other marketing and corporate personnel.

Ames[7] has emphasised that the product-manager system should take 'well-earned bows' for the success of many outstanding companies. The system makes possible vigorous product-by-product leadership, and the many instances where it is obviously working well suggests that the concept is basically sound. Moreover, Mancuso[8] suggests that product managers have a greater market impact than is often realised; indeed they are instrumental in creating company 'image' by reason of their activities in markets.

RESPONSIBILITIES OF THE PRODUCT MANAGER

It will be useful at this point to distinguish those areas of responsibility commonly associated with the adoption of product managers.

In a paper given at the 45th National Conference of the American Marketing Association, William S. Callander[9] noted seven major areas of responsibility commonly associated with the product manager. These may usefully be reduced into the following groupings.

Planning. The forces of technological innovation which gave birth to the product-manager system simultaneously confront it with its greatest challenge – anticipation of change and the preparation of plans and techniques to cope effectively with this change.

Information-seeking and Evaluation. In order to anticipate change it is necessary continually to scan the business environment and monitor the strength and direction of relevant trends. Specifically this involves keeping track of competitors' activity in the widest sense, that is one must not merely keep informed of directly competing substitutes but must attempt to identify the less-immediate threat implicit in new products and processes. Equally one must be sensitive to marketing innovations as, for example, the adoption of systems selling, and so forth.

Co-ordination. As the 'product' expert it is the product manager's responsibility to co-ordinate the efforts of all those company functions which impinge upon the successful marketing of that product. Of all his responsibilities it is this which presents the greatest challenge, requiring the product manager to be, in effect, all things to all men.

Control. This function incorporates not only price/cost and budgetary dimensions but also extends into the introduction of new products and the phasing-out of old products.

Although the four areas listed above are a valid indication of the product manager's sphere of responsibility, no useful generalisation can be made of their relative importance as, of necessity, this will vary from firm to firm. Mancuso does, however, suggest that where product managers are used they will 'at least' be responsible for the following:

(1) product strategy, including pricing;
(2) capital expenditures and budgets;
(3) sales forecasting;
(4) advertising and promotional effort;
(5) preparing and interpreting product reports; and
(6) trouble-shooting.

This writer then suggests that for 'committed companies' – thereby implying a kind of gradation of intensity of application of the system – the list can be extended to include:

(7) product profit-and-loss responsibility;
(8) direct control over engineering and technical development of the product;
(9) purchasing and 'quality control' related to the product; and
(10) new product responsibility for related products.

That it is impossible to lay down general guidelines as to the relative importance of different facets of the product manager's responsibilities is implicit in the findings of a survey of metalworking firms by *Steel*.[10]

In answer to the question, 'Which single function do you consider most important in the product manager's job?', the following pattern emerged:

	Per cent
Sales	31·3
Product planning – marketing	28·1
Profits	21·9
Product R and D	7·8
Scheduling and expediting	3·1
Other functions	7·8

Although conceived essentially as a marketing function, the question, 'Where do your product managers report?', elicited the following responses:

	Per cent
Sales and marketing	71·9
Division manager	7·8
President	4·7
Engineering manager	3·1
Material control	3·1
Product planning	1·6
Other functions	7·8

THE PRODUCT-MANAGER SYSTEM IN PRACTICE

Although, as suggested above, many firms have enjoyed benefits from the product-manager system, this experience has by no means been widespread. Indeed, the dissatisfaction with the system experienced by many companies has led to a lively debate as to the root causes and possible remedies. It is intended to turn to some of these issues now.

In the opinion of one authority much of the disillusionment expressed about the product-manager concept is directly attributable to attempts 'to generalize from successful company experience'.[11] The truth of this contention may be inferred from the reasons advanced by companies for dropping the system and from the title of an article in *Sales Management* which seeks to deal with this phenomenon – 'Has the Product Manager Failed? OR The Folly of Imitation'.[12]

Another factor put forward by this observer is what is described as failure to abide by a basic management precept, namely that responsibility should be accompanied by authority. Although product-manager responsibility will vary from firm to firm, experience suggests that, in general, his authority is not commensurate with it. This is seen as particularly disturbing in the light of certain unique characteristics of the product manager's position in the company. The product manager does not have line responsibility in the classic sense, nor does he perform a staff function in the sense of support staff (for example in market research). However, he *does* serve as a focal point for planning and co-ordinating the profitable growth of products. He is therefore, according to Ames, an 'organisational anomaly' requiring special treatment which he all too often does not get.

At least the product manager should expect comprehensive support from the organisation as a whole to perform what is acknowledged to be a uniquely difficult task. However, Luck and Novak suggest that rather than support, the product manager is more likely to find himself constrained by the organisation.[13] They summarise the following organisational constraints:

(1) not all functions (market research, sales, and so on) give him adequate information;

(2) his resources in terms of clerical and other assistance may be so limited that he is kept desk-bound pre-occupied with planning and with inadequate time to consider alternative strategies;

(3) he may not be adequately involved in product development and so may be made responsible for poor products that others have developed – therefore he should be closely involved in new-product development from the start;

(4) he must receive support in order to ensure that objectives (for example advertising) are met – also he needs feedback of information on the marketing effort;

(5) and (6) under these headings the authors allude to the problem of authority and responsibility mentioned above.

In those companies which have persevered with the product-manager concept it is clear that success is rarely immediate and is dependent upon a number of factors among which a flexible attitude at all levels of management is a necessary and enabling factor. However, before turning to a consideration of factors likely to promote the successful operation of the system, it may be useful to outline some of the reasons why it may fail.

Ames takes the view that the fundamental fault lies with top management in their failure to apply 'a basically sound management tool'.[14] Admittedly product management is not the easiest organisational arrangement to apply. But breakdowns of the system can none the less be traced to fundamental failures on the part of senior management. They can be listed, following Ames, under the following headings.

(1) *Off-the-shelf approach.* By this is meant a piecemeal approach to the system, resulting in inadequate consideration of the product manager's specific requirements, failure to spell out specifically his responsibility and authority, and, advertently or inadvertently, cutting him off from adequate liaison with essential interfaces.

(2) *Expecting too much.* The product manager's job is likened by Ames, not without exaggeration to 'walking blindfold on a treadmill'. He is expected, single-handed, to resolve a whole rag-bag of management problems, for example high manufacturing costs, late deliveries, and so on. Thus the product manager is liable to be blamed for virtually anything that goes wrong with a product, while in many instances the fault will lie elsewhere.

(3) *Expecting too little.* Here management's fault may be to allow the product-manager system to degenerate into low-level clerical activity with inadequate responsibility and status.

(4) *Assigning the wrong man.* Ames's view is that the system will not work 'with anything less than outstanding men' occupying product-manager positions. More than anyone else he influences the destiny of his product. All others have functional responsibility, but only he has a full-time commitment to the product.

MANAGING THE PRODUCT MANAGER'S INTERFACES

It is clear that the foregoing weaknesses are largely ascribed by Ames to inadequacy on the part of senior management. However, given the constraints imposed by managements, what avenues are open to the product manager to improve performance by his own efforts? Perhaps the major area susceptible to improvement is that of dealing with his numerous interfaces, in that even in an atmosphere of inadequate top-management support, productive associations should, in theory at least, be fostered by improvements in the product manager's human-relations skills. Clearly, an ability to solicit support from others in the organisation is likely to be an important factor in determining whether a product manager succeeds or fails. To put the matter another way, what are the interpersonal barriers faced by product managers in obtaining interface support, and how might these be overcome?

This issue has been addressed by Gemmill and Wilemon[15] who suggest that what they call an 'influence matrix' exists in product management consisting of four basic types of influence:

(1) *Reward power* – an ability to induce interfaces to comply with a product manager's requests because they perceive him as being capable of directly or indirectly dispensing rewards;

(2) *Punishment power* – an ability to induce interfaces to comply with a product manager's requests because they perceive him as being able directly or indirectly to dispense punishments for non-compliance;

(3) *Expert power* – an ability to induce interfaces to comply with a product manager's requests because of their respect for his marketing judgement and skills;

(4) *Referent power* – an ability to induce interfaces to comply with a product manager's requests because they identify with him, have friendship ties with him, or respect his position within the company.

The two writers stress that product managers in general find themselves deficient under all of these headings. Taken together with the weaknesses described in the previous section, it is little wonder that a major thrust of product-management literature in recent years has been towards offering prescriptive remedies of various types. It is to some of these remedies that we now turn, and to preserve the continuity of the chapter let us first of all consider the remedies open to product managers finding themselves deficient in reward, punishment, expert and referent power. Thereafter we may consider the much larger top-management issues.

PRESCRIPTIVE REMEDIES

(1) *Overcoming interpersonal barriers*

Deficiencies in reward power. An interface, for example an engineering manager capable of providing valuable technical support to product managers, may decline to give support because 'there's just no percentage in it for me'.[16] In other words, the engineering manager, to pursue the example, perceives the product manager as being unable to give him direct compensation by way of, for example, salary increase or promotion power. In this case the product manager may be supported because he is perceived as being in a high-status position with access to and support of senior management. If he is not so perceived then his indirect reward power is diminished.

Faced with deficiencies in reward power, Gemmill and Wilemon point to certain courses of action open to the product manager. For example, he may attempt to increase his accessibility to top management which could increase his perceived indirect power. In more drastic cases he may even 'bluff' interfaces in terms of top-management support for his product line and in terms of the rewards he can dispense.

Deficiences in punishment power. Generally, product managers are unable to apply any sanctions to interfaces unwilling to accede to their requests for assistance. On the other hand, many product managers do have indirect punishment power in the sense that they are capable of feeding negative evaluations about interfaces to those who are officially empowered to make evaluative recommendations. In theory, such power can be enhanced by making adverse comments about interfaces to senior management, but the drawbacks of such an approach in terms of souring his relations with interfaces are obvious.

Deficiences in expert power. A major problem facing the product manager is to convince interfaces of his expert knowledge of the job. For example, he needs to gain the sales department's respect for his marketing judgement, the advertising agent's respect for his communications knowledge, and so on. Clearly this is a formidable task even for an experienced product manager, and in practice many product managers and their assistants are relatively young. There is an obvious role to be played here by senior management, but equally there is much the product manager can do himself to improve his understanding and expertise in areas where interface problems are most critical.

Deficiencies in referent power. In this case the product manager has three main courses open to him. First, he can try to cultivate friendship ties with critical interfaces. Second, he can try to increase his understanding of problems faced by crucial interfaces, this leading to a feeling that he truly shares the problems of the interfaces. Finally, he can seek to improve his marketing expertise and track record in making good decisions. Gemmill and Wilemon argue that this might induce interfaces to support him because of personal attraction to him and admiration of him as a model.

A general comment. Generally Gemmill and Wilemon take the view that expert power tends to be the most desirable form of influence. The use of reward and punishment power suffers from a number of limitations,[17] including the stimulation of defensiveness on the part of interfaces, and perhaps poor motivation of interfaces in that they will tend to allocate their efforts on the basis of the good or harm they think the product manager can do them, rather than on what is best for the organisation. Equally, referent power suffers limitations, not least that personal loyalty to a product manager may override loyalty to the organisation.

Support for the view that expert power is likely to be the most desirable form of influence the product manager can use is provided by Lawrence and Lorsch.[18] In a study of integrators such as product managers they found that those in more effective organisations tended to be more influential in obtaining interface support because of their expertise while those in less effective organisations were only influential because of the formal authority and sanctions associated with their positions.

(2) *Top-Management Correctives*

Among the writers who have most cogently urged a different approach to product management by top management are Ames, Luck, and Luck and Novak.[19] In that some of the points made by each author are similar it may be useful to offer a summary of the major considerations put forward by all three writers. This is done below. The points reflect the actions these writers feel senior management should take to improve the operation of the product-manager system.

Establishment of the need for product management. This point is a straightforward one: given that other organisational approaches are possible, top management has a responsibility to ensure that the correct form is used. This may not be product managers, but perhaps market managers, or conventional sales managers.

Adherence to fundamental organisational principles. Here Ames makes a plea for not burying a product manager in organisational layers.[20] His specific activities and working relationships need to be spelled out, preferably in writing (see the 'job specification' laid out in Table 5.1).

TABLE 5.1   *Job Specification for a product manager*

Because of the nature of the product manager's job, his responsibility must be defined in more detail than might otherwise be necessary. This is important not only to guide the product manager, but also to familiarise others in the organisation with what management expects of the product manager. The two following examples contrast descriptions of the product manager's role and relationships with one area – product development.

Here is a typical statement taken from a major company that offers inadequate guidance to the product manager:

> *Statement of responsibility*: Works closely with product development to ensure adequate plans and programmes for his product line.

Now, here is the kind of statement that does provide the product manager with a basis for achieving understanding and building close working relationships. It is taken from the product manager's position description in another company which, understandably, has been outstanding in its use of this concept:

The critical importance of new-product development in the company's business cannot be overemphasised. It is the mainstream for product improvements and new applications so vital to the company's continuing growth and profitability.

The product development department is responsible basically for developing and testing new products and applications and for improving existing products and processes. The relationships of product managers with this department will be centred on the product development manager who is responsible for his assigned product line. The basic responsibility for recommending applications and product development goals and programmes rests with the product development manager. However in order to ensure a marketing-oriented point of view, the product development manager should rely heavily on the counsel of the product manager in determining the general nature of projects for his product line and the priorities that should be assigned to them.

An important responsibility of the product manager is to guide the efforts of the product development groups into the most profitable channels from a sales standpoint. He does this by keeping these groups closely informed of field needs, important market trends, and his own marketing plans. In effect, the product manager supplies the major part of the commercial intelligence needed by the product development department.

Ultimately, the director of product development and the vice-president of marketing must collaborate in establishing the total applications and product development goals of the company, the over-all budget for this activity, and the priorities of major products.

Once project priorities and timetables are established, the product manager is expected to incorporate product development plans for his product line into his over-all product plans. And he is charged with the responsibility for keeping informed on the general status of projects for his product line and seeing that appropriate corrective action is taken when schedules bog down or planned goals are not achieved. To this end, he directs the discussions related to his product line in regularly scheduled development meetings and takes the initiative to secure the involvement of other departments when that is necessary.

Source: Ames, 'Pay-off from Product Management', *Harvard Business Review*, vol. 41 (Nov–Dec 1963).

Luck and Novak urge that he needs 'definite authority', specifically supervisory (command over personnel) and prescriptive (the power to command resources, subject to senior-management approval). This authority would be commensurate with specific responsibilities laid down by top management.

Development of a manning 'specification' that is realistically geared to the range of skills required to conduct product-management tasks. The point here is that different product managers need different skills, ranging from the advertising skill of the packaged-goods company product manager, to the technical skills of the industrial-goods product manager. What is needed is a comprehensive checklist to evaluate the skills necessary for the job. Such a checklist would have to include factors such as demonstrable sense of business judgement and different personal skills appropriate to managing various interfaces and dealing with a varied assortment of problems. Ideally such a list would be used as a basis for formal evaluation of product-manager performance.

Provision for comprehensive training. While the product manager's function does not lend itself to training so easily as in the case of, for example, field-sales personnel, Ames believes that the effort can and should be made, and he gives the example of one company who provide the product manager with a list of specific first steps he should take when beginning an assignment. These are:

(1) study all literature connected with the product-manager position;
(2) obtain the view of the vice-president (marketing) on management of the product line;
(3) become familiar with the company's marketing planning and control processes;
(4) ensure enough product information is available; and
(5) develop a written marketing plan for the product group.

Subsequently, the product manager is coached on the fundamentals of planning and on the 'how to' aspects of the job, including promotional planning. Ames argues strongly that training is possible and that firms would get more out of the system were they to indulge in this activity.

Provision of a 'better atmosphere' to study markets and alternative strategies. In this case Luck[21] is concerned that, because of inadequate resources the product manager has little time to study alternative strategies in terms of pricing, promotion, distribution and other areas.

CONCLUSION

Although the role of the product manager has been subject to scrutiny in this chapter, it is as well to remind ourselves in conclusion that this is only one organisational form available to managements when considering how best to manage products. Company experience suggests that it is 'here to stay' but is only one means of improving product-marketing performance. Other possibilities, for example market managers and sales managers, were mentioned in the chapter. Moreover, if we take the case of market managers, it is apparent that they have similar interface, authority, responsibility, and other problems, the only significant operational difference being that the product manager is responsible for servicing a single product (perhaps in many markets) while the market manager services a single market (perhaps with many products).

Perhaps the major point to hold to is that correct organisational design. whatever form it takes, is fundamental to marketing success. Product managers are undoubtedly the correct choice in many instances, as are market managers in others. That the task each faces is in general a daunting one should not deter them from making strenuous efforts to improve their efficiency, nor should it deter managements from creating the best climate for their operations.

Chapter 6

The New-Product Development Process

INTRODUCTION

The previous chapter highlighted the problems of the management of products, with particular emphasis on the role of product and market managers. It was noted that the latter had numerous responsibilities, not least among these being an interest in new products. However, because of the numerous interfaces dealt with, there was the likelihood that some of these relationships might not be developed in depth.

It is clear, however, that regardless of how much time the product or market manager can devote to new-product matters, as distinct from managing an existing line, the firm as a whole cannot afford to neglect this area, representing, as it does, a major facet of product planning. It is to this subject that we now turn in greater detail.

Before developing the topic it is as well to record that not all firms regard the internal development 'route' to new products as the sole means of attaining product objectives. Growth may, for example, take place through licensing arrangements with individuals or firms who have themselves conceived and perhaps developed a new idea. Indeed, some firms develop a capability to exploit licences which itself may emerge as a major source of company strength. Licence arrangements are of various sorts and may, for example, be a purely sales licence, with the licensor retaining control of production. On the other hand, the licence may be for an idea not fully developed, so that the licensee is obliged to conduct additional R and D to refine the idea.

In addition to licensing, the firm may choose to expand through merger or acquisition. This may be seen by managements as a rather less complicated and costly means of obtaining a foothold in a newer market, than internal technical development. Once again the ability to seek out and quickly assess profitable acquisition possibilities may, with experience, develop into a major dimension of a firm's expertise.

It is as well to remember, too, that while a firm may pursue new-product development as a deliberate policy, this need not imply any neglect of the existing range. Indeed, attention to new and existing products will go hand in hand. As far as the existing range is concerned, the firm may do various things. For example, studies may be initiated to seek out new markets and new applications; improved market feedback systems may be installed to generate market reaction to product design, the information being used as an input to the design office for possible product redesign; finally, the package may be kept under close scrutiny, with possible redesign to achieve better market impact or to invade newer markets.

With these reservations in mind, we may now turn to an examination of the new-product development process, including a consideration of organisational issues posed by the process.

NEW-PRODUCT EVOLUTIONARY CYCLE

The stages through which new products evolve were summarised at a recent conference as follows: 'We follow normally six steps: idea generation; screening; business appraisal; physical development; testing, and finally commercialisation.'[1]

This breakdown of activities is widely accepted. Thus Booz, Allen and Hamilton, in their investigations of the new-product activities of several hundred companies find that regardless of type of company, industry or product, there are six fairly clear phases or stages in the evolutionary cycle.[2] These phases are called (1) 'exploration', (2) 'screening', (3) 'business analysis', (4) 'development', (5) 'testing', and (6) 'commercialisation'.

As an idea or product moves through the development

process, a decision whether to proceed or reject is called for at the culmination of each stage. The commercial (or market-launch) stage provides the transition from the evolutionary cycle itself to the starting-point of the product's life cycle. The stage needs to be included here because many of the decisions called for during commercialisation are based upon planning during previous stages. Commercialisation is also the phase where marketing is most active in connection with the new product.

In analysing the process of innovation in terms of component parts it is not intended to give unqualified support to the view that innovation is necessarily an orderly and predictable process. A methodical, step-by-step approach is, however, of use in that it provides a logical framework for analysis. This is used here. Also, let it be stressed that some aspects of the innovatory process can only be performed in sequence, for example commercialisation cannot precede design, development and manufacture of the product.

However, we shall approach cautiously some of the more extreme rational views of innovation, in particular the inherent assumption of orderliness, the assumption that uncertainty is necessarily reduced progressively throughout the process, the assumption that projects can be cut off neatly at predetermined checkpoints, and the assumption that successful innovation is dependent upon the institution of formal, sequential procedures.

With these provisos in mind we now move to a brief discussion of the major elements in the evolutionary cycle. The main purpose of this is to give a broad outline of the areas to be covered in more detail later.

IDEA GENERATION

The first stage of the new product's evolution begins with an idea for the product. Ideas can originate from many sources and their scope can range from small improvements to radically new products. The company cannot afford to underestimate the importance of maintaining and stimulating a flow of new ideas. The creation of new products is a condition of survival in many industries. Failure to keep abreast of competition, in terms of new products, means that the company's product-mix becomes obsolete and hence unsaleable. What is needed, therefore, is an adequate stockpile of ideas which are directed to appropriate executives for examination and evaluation. Not all ideas will have immediate market potential of course, and it is for this reason that some firms will file patent claims on particular discoveries to ensure exclusive rights if the item later proves to possess commercial possibilities.

It is tempting to form the belief that idea generation should be the subject of set procedures established deliberately within the firm and that the process itself should be programmed and managed to produce results desired by management. Pessemier states that 'Unless the search process is so organised that it brings to management's attention those products which are likely to return a substantial profit, a new product programme cannot function effectively.'[3]

While we support the need for a systematic approach to this and other stages of new product development, it will nevertheless be stressed that idea generation may at times defy formal organisation and may even be stifled by it. One should note also Pessemier's emphasis on future profitability. At this very early stage in the evolutionary cycle, such estimates are bound to be crude. Indeed, insistence upon them may unnecessarily restrict creative thought. On the other hand, firms are advised to explore the potentialities of technological forecasting, discussed in Chapter 4, as an input to new-product thinking.

Pessemier's quotation states a management ideal, the desirability of whose attainment few would dispute. To suggest that success will automatically follow the institution of predetermined organisational arrangements is not always at one with company experience.

IDEA SCREENING

Once ideas have been solicited and collected they need to be subjected to a sifting process to eliminate those inconsistent with the product policies and objectives of the firm. Some ideas may be obvious non-starters and may be dropped after the application of only rough screening criteria. For example, an idea may be of little use because it is already protected by patent, or because raw material supplies for its eventual manufacture are too difficult to obtain or are too costly. Other ideas will hold out more promise, and, if they survive the initial rough screening stage, can be subjected to more detailed examination involving the use of a variety of screening criteria. The use of such measures is dictated by the need for an objective basis upon which to judge whether the idea is worthy of further consideration or whether it should be eliminated. This stage frequently also demands further elaboration in order that the full product concept can be visualised. The major implications of the potential new product to the firm can be identified. The main intention of this phase, it can be emphasised, is to eliminate unsuitable ideas as quickly as possible.

The development of formal screening procedures in recent years has led to the belief in some quarters that these are obligatory to managements in the process of reducing the uncertainty surrounding new product proposals. It seems logical to view new products as entering a detailed screening process at the termination of which sufficient certainty exists to enable management to select a group of very promising possibilities. In reality, screening may merely provide a useful framework for analysing a new-product proposal, but may do little to reduce uncertainty to acceptable levels. At this early stage in the firm's enquiries, data about the potential of the product may be crude, leaving the go/no-go decision to be determined on the basis of managerial experience and judgement.

IDEA EVALUATION

The ideas that 'pass' detailed screening can now be scrutinised in depth, with particular emphasis on the technical feasibility and likely profitability of the proposed new product. Judgements made at this stage will only be as accurate as available information allows. The decision facing management is basically one of determining, if possible, the likely rate of return on investment that can be expected from the new product. Although rate of return in monetary terms is the major objective, other considerations may influence management's final decision. These include strengthening the product line, gaining access to new markets for the whole product line, and establishing a reputation for technical competence. This stage normally yields a planning document – the development proposal – which, if accepted by management, lays down the course of action the company will undertake to develop the product and prepare it for eventual market introduction. The importance of this phase in the evolutionary cycle cannot be understated because subsequent stages begin to incur heavy costs, and many potential failures can be eliminated at this stage providing the decision taken is based upon factually sound information.

It is at the stage of financial evaluation that management's desire for detailed quantified information is at its most intense, and at this point there is the hope that perhaps quite sophisticated investment-appraisal techniques can be applied to sound quantified data. In practice, even at this point, the desired information may be absent and there may be no prospect of obtaining it. Also, some firms may be sceptical of the value of financial techniques and may make their decisions on other criteria. There is also a belief in some firms that even very exhaustive cost and revenue data will not reduce uncertainty to adequate levels. This reflects the view that there is a point in new-product decisions beyond which financial evaluation cannot go. It is in this atmosphere that decisions may require to be taken.

TECHNICAL DEVELOPMENT

Technical development is the phase in the evolutionary cycle which normally requires the greatest amount of time to complete. It is during this period that all development of the product, from idea to final physical form, takes place. The technical portions of the development proposal must be broken into individual projects and assignments for R and D personnel to accomplish. As technical setbacks take place product specifications and final product form may require to be revised. During the long time span necessary to accomplish technical development the conditions underlying the development may change – for example, a rival may introduce a similar product to the market more quickly, or government economic policy might force a cut-back in business spending, thus changing the market outlook. These and various other conditions may force technical revisions of the new products, and at worst may prompt the firm to cease the development.

Based on the foregoing, there is a tendency to assume that the major decisions facing managements during development are those concerned with cancelling or proceeding with projects.[4] It should not be doubted that these are problems of great significance for management. What should be questioned, however, is the assumption that the procedure is a straight-forward one, in particular that once a 'no-go' situation has been reached, cancellation is automatic. In reality, the firm may build up a progressive commitment such that the project acquires a momentum of its own, capable of defying well-documented and perhaps quantified arguments for termination.

During technical development, too, it seems logical to argue, as we did in Chapter 4, in favour of a continuing audit of the marketing and other factors which originally favoured initiation of the project. In this way marketing is seen as constantly monitoring changes in the external environment, and feeding these to technical staff, so that the project can be modified or abandoned if necessary. The assumption that a project will in practice be dropped on receipt of adverse information was queried above. It can be added that the conduct of market-research studies during development encounters the same problems as pre-development studies: it may not prove possible to reduce uncertainty significantly. Management may therefore be obliged to depend upon their own interpretation of the environment.

TESTING

Once technical development is complete the next phase involves measurement of the product's likely market acceptability through technical and market testing. The object of this stage is basically to assess whether the product meets the technical and commercial objectives envisaged in the original development proposal, or as amended as a result of commercial and technical changes taking place during development. There are normally two aspects of the testing stage, these being to some extent interrelated. They are: (i) testing the product itself to ensure that it meets intended physical specifications, and, (ii) testing the new product to ensure that it will meet the commercial specifications upon which it is based.

Although test-marketing objectives may be stated readily enough, the practical problems of achieving them are formidable in reality. The notion that test marketing provides a neat solution to problems of likely market acceptability of the product is not always borne out in practice. One problem which may be mentioned briefly here is the manner in which technology and need interact. The appearance and successful operation of the first prototype may lead potential users to seek more involved applications for the product, this leading to a progressive modification of the original specification. Not only may it be difficult to assess consumer need in advance, but this need is a function of the product and may change when the product is available at the testing stage.

COMMERCIALISATION

It is at this stage that the product is first submitted to the market and so commences its life cycle. Clearly this market-introduction stage is a critical one for any new product and needs to be handled skilfully. Much of the work to be conducted at this point has to be planned at earlier stages of the evolutionary cycle if the transition is to be made effectively.

A detailed study of new-product commercialisation problems is beyond the scope of this book. Such an analysis would necessarily lead to examination of such areas as marketing-mix selection, optimisation of mix elements, and would ideally consider factors influencing the rate of diffusion of innovations.

Despite the care with which the previous development stages have been planned, unforeseen events, over which the firm has no control, can impair commercialisation seriously. Also the success of this stage is closely related to more volatile activities such as advertising and personal selling, whose effectiveness may be difficult to quantify.

CHARACTERISTICS OF THE EVOLUTIONARY CYCLE

As might be expected the stages of the evolutionary cycle vary in importance from one product to another. For example, the technical-development stage is neither as lengthy, nor perhaps as critical, for some types of consumer goods such as, say, a new brand of soap, as against a highly technical product such as a new machine tool. Also, within the stages themselves the problems encountered by different product types are normally dissimilar. Thus the problems of market testing a new brand of cigarette, to give an example from the consumer-goods field, are different from those encountered in the case of a new welding machine.

Despite the relative importance of each stage, and the different emphasis between stages, all new-product development, regardless of product, appears to fit, with greater or lesser degrees of precision, within the stages outlined. It is true that the firm may or may not recognise the phases explicitly, but necessary decisions do require to be taken at each of the stages. In the interests of better management practice in an area of such importance the recognition of these stages in the new-product evolutionary cycle has a contribution to make towards reducing the rate of new-product failures and the concomitant wastage of scarce resources.

The evolutionary process is, to some extent, sequential, each stage following upon the other. While this is convenient for analytical purposes, it is not necessarily always true in practice. Thus, as mentioned earlier, commercialisation plans have to be actively considered at stages prior to the actual launch of the product. In addition, if unforeseen difficulties emerge in solving engineering problems associated with the development, the entire procedure may require to feed back to the starting-point and begin anew. To illustrate, production-engineering difficulties encountered at the prototype building stage may have their root in a design deficiency, for example failure to design for maximum use of standard parts. This could lead to reference back to the design office.

Having said something in outline about the evolutionary cycle of new products, what can be said about the organisational implications of the process? This is dealt with below.

ORGANISATION OF NEW-PRODUCT DEVELOPMENT – THE NEED FOR INTEGRATION

There is ample support for the view that successful innovation is most likely to result from integrating the various steps of the new-product evolutionary cycle.

Berenson addresses the problem of the transference of R and D results to the market-place and makes proposals for quickening this process.[5] Among these proposals is a strong plea for improved organisation. Berenson conceptualises the innovatory process as a system divisible into three major 'sub-systems', the R and D department, the marketing department, and the market. Innovation can thus be thought of in terms of directing the transfer of ideas from one sub-system to another across interfaces. (A similar idea has been put forward by Ansoff and Stewart.[6] They propose the idea of 'downstream coupling'. By this is meant the extent to which the product's introduction depends upon communication and co-operation between R and D, manufacturing and marketing, all further 'downstream' towards the end user. The authors argue that knowledge of 'coupling requirement' and its proper management can avert the frictions commonly encountered at the marketing/engineering interface.)

Berenson suggests five methods of increasing what he calls movement across the interfaces.

The first he introduces only to dismiss. This is a proposal for a unilateral increase in resource input at the R and D 'end'. He rejects this on the grounds that the mere act of increasing expenditure will not in itself guarantee results. Few

D

will dispute this conclusion. In any case the suggestion does not seem practicable.

The second proposal is for a 'faster rate of transference of results' from sub-systems two and three, thus creating 'energy' for replacement. Under this heading the author advocates more rigorous product-mix-profitability studies so that unsuccessful products are deleted from the range. Also urged is greater discrimination on the part of the marketing department in that they should be more willing to reject unsatisfactory suggestions emanating from R and D. In plain language, Berenson is urging an 'unclogging' of the system, both in terms of products already on the market and also of proposed new products, in the belief that this will produce the necessary pressures to fill the gaps with profitable products. The author does not elaborate on how this pressure is meant to operate in order to produce the desired results.

The final three points bring us more firmly into the area of organisation.

The third proposal is for an increase in the activity of the sub-systems. Berenson points out that the transfer of technology in a firm is assisted by organisation, in particular organisational arrangements for co-ordinating the total process of bringing R and D results to the market-place. One example given is that of project teams charged with 'seeing the whole job through'. Another is product managers, though where one such manager is alone responsible for the co-ordination task difficulties arise partly because of the wide knowledge required and partly because of the various interfaces that have to be surmounted.

The fourth and fifth proposals may be merged for the sake of brevity. These urge the importance of increasing the area of contact between R and D and marketing, hopefully thereby improving the perception of R and D by sub-systems two and three. Job mobility is put forward as a possible means of reducing friction between sub-systems.

This theme of integration and its importance in the organisation of innovation is taken up by Lawrence and Lorsch.[7] What is required, according to these authors, is an 'integrator' – a separate functionary who integrates the innovatory idea into the on-going operation it is designed to serve. Two types of integrating procedures are generally employed – separate organisational entities such as market-development departments, or new-product departments; or temporary groups such as the project team or the cross-functional committee.

Ward addresses himself to the same problem.[8] He approaches it by stressing that the future of a company, involving innovation and new products, is at least as important as its present. Present and future are, however, 'inevitably in conflict' and are the 'key dichotomy' which should be recognised in company structure.

The nature of this dichotomy has been stressed by Levitt.[9] He states that 'They [R and D departments and long-range planning departments] are implicit recognitions that an organisation that exists to get today's job done cannot also do tomorrow's job very well. Tomorrow's job needs a new structural entity, a diminutive autonomous organisation of its own.'

Levitt's point is that the objective of business organisation is to achieve a specific purpose, that is the efficient exercise of day-to-day activities such as direction of the sales force and the control of the plant. Thus, 'Allegiance to the daily task remains the predominant and inevitable focus.' Within such a constraining context, Levitt argues, it is difficult to focus also on innovating activity because this is essentially disruptive; 'there develops an almost inescapable clash with the prevailing organisational creed'. Accordingly, the creation of entirely new products (and indeed new businesses or markets) argues the institution of separate organisational arrangements.

Ward proposes an approach designed to redress the balance of corporate activity in favour of the future (See Figure 6.1).[10] Reporting to the chief executive are two general managers (or vice-presidents) of equal status, one concerned with day-to-day activities, the other with the future. To the general manager (present) report the normal line functions of a business; to the general manager (future) report the market-planning and technical-research departments. To the extent that the future cannot be predicted with accuracy, this is a plea for the need for managerial intuition in long-range planning.

There is the problem of where one is to assume the 'future' begins. Ward's proposals in this connection are not entirely

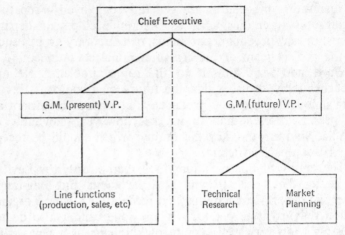

FIG. 6.1. *Organigram for change*

satisfactory in that he proposes that no line need in fact be drawn between the present and the future. One general manager is to be concerned with the efficient running of present operations, the other for seeing that desirable change is introduced. Ward allows that overlap of responsibility is bound to occur, but agrees that, at least in his proposal, any conflict would be explicit rather than latent or submerged.

The proposed structure is also consistent, the author argues, with project or task-force approaches to launching new-product developments. The 'future' management structure would be responsible for new product proposals at their embryonic stage. When successful market introduction appears possible, they may be transferred, perhaps with appropriate project staff, to the 'present' side, or possibly set up as a joint venture. Indeed, with Berenson, Ward urges the desirability of job mobility not only between R and D and marketing, but also between present and future structures.

It seems to the writers that these proposals may create more problems than they resolve. Insisting that R and D and marketing departments report to the same general manager will not solve deeply rooted interface problems overnight. Also, Ward does seem to minimise the fact that his proposals involve the creation of a further interface which may not have existed explicitly before, that is a 'present–future' interface.

Another point is that all firms need to consider long- and short-term matters, even if no explicit organisational arrangements are made.

It is not very helpful, however, to offer purely destructive criticism. Judging by the literature, examples of which are cited above, and also by field research, many companies appear still to be at an experimental stage – if they have experimented at all – as far as organisation of innovatory activity is concerned. Anomalies are bound to emerge and mistakes be made. It is against this background that one must judge new organisational proposals, and the performance of any one company or group of companies.

PROBLEMS OF ORGANISATION IN PRACTICE

In stressing the importance of integrating the different stages of new-product development, we would wish to avoid creating the impression of having 'found the answer' to innovational organisation. In many ways, emphasis on integration merely states an obvious management ideal, moreover it does little to solve the practical problems of companies having to achieve it in real life. In particular, major innovations pose quite frightening problems of organisation, as, for example, Schon has observed.[11]

Schon states that it is true that where innovations are marginal (for example new package design or slightly different fabric weave) development can be orderly, predictable and subject to strict control. On the other hand, when one is dealing with innovations such as transistors or television, major changes in technology are involved which demand new concepts of marketing and marketing organisation, as well as radically different production equipment. In such circumstances, Schon states, innovating firms face major organisational changes, frequently in unpredictable directions. There is, therefore, much in the process of innovation which defies conventional management planning and the application of 'systematic programmes' for new-product development.

There is, however, a disturbing tendency to assume that innovation is sufficiently similar to other company functions to enable it to be controlled by means of such activities as improved planning, clearer objectives, better co-ordination of effort, and improved market knowledge. Thus, the two major weaknesses in the management of new products have been suggested by one study to be the following:

1. Failure to recognise and adopt a systematic programme for new-product development. The most frequently incurred problems in this regard, in order of their frequency, are the following:
   (a) lack of appropriate planning activity
   (b) lack of objectives
   (c) failure to appraise markets, and
   (d) lack of a system to gather ideas.
2. Inadequate implementation and execution of the new product programme. Problems most frequently experienced here include:
   (a) poor organisation and co-ordination of effort
   (b) poor control over schedules and cost
   (c) inadequate personnel
   (d) lack of innovation, and
   (e) poor execution of the new product programme.[12]

This view has an obvious appeal to anyone confronted with the complex task of developing new technology in an organisational setting within fixed boundaries of time and resources; in some circumstances it may even appear an obligatory view. Also there are obvious benefits accruing to formal planning. For example, the formulation of objectives for technical effort provides direction for the effort, even if these objectives have to be modified in the light of discoveries made in the process. Also, there is value in mapping out stages in the development process and identifying major checkpoints, even if in practice preconceived development plans subsequently require radical revision.

There is, however, as Schon emphasises, much in the process of innovation which defies conventional management planning. Nevertheless, it is a common assumption that improved performance in the new-product area should be sought precisely by applying systematic programmes for new-product development. Such programmes would be most likely to be found flourishing in what Burns[13] has called 'management-centred' organisations in contradistinction to 'enterprise-centred' ones, yet it is in the latter, not the former, within which, in Burns's view, innovation is most likely to flourish. Let us develop this argument briefly.

By management-centred organisation Burns means a situation where the company's tasks are broken down into specialisms each pursued for its own sake while the head of the concern is responsible for seeing to the relevance of each task, that is the head is assumed to be the sole repository of knowledge of the firm's situation and tasks. Interaction between management levels tends to be vertical, with information flowing 'downwards'. What we have here is the type of command hierarchy familiar in company-organisation charts. In the case of entrepreneur-centred organisations, problems and needs cannot be broken down into specialisms within a closely defined hierarchy. Rather than relying upon the head of the concern for direction emanating vertically, individuals are obliged to perform their specialised functions in the light of their knowledge of the tasks of the firm as a whole. Interaction runs laterally rather than vertically and has more the characteristic of lateral consultation than vertical command. In such a situation, tasks are more difficult to define as they require constant redefinition in the light of communication with others participating in the task. Finally, the head of the concern is no longer thought of as the sole possessor of knowledge of the firm's situation and its tasks.

In essence, Burns is arguing that the innovative process, demanding, as it does, much cross-functional activity as well as a high level of creative thinking, is in principle identical with the function of the classical entrepreneur, and that the task of organising industrial science is simply to facilitate technical entrepreneurship.

Broad support for this plea for flexibility of organisational structure in providing a favourable atmosphere for technological innovation has been given by Shanks. He notes that innovation has flourished 'where there is a certain fluidity and flexibility in the company structure, which permits the interplay of personality and ideas, and where management is psychologically ready to alter existing plans to accommodate change and innovation'.[14]

The importance of human and organisational factors in technological innovation has led to more strenuous efforts to improve the management of information by changing organisational structure. Venture teams, new-product committees and business development departments are examples. In the case of venture management,[15] for example, one individual is made responsible for the project in charge of a full-time team, thus creating the advantages of a 'small firm' environment, namely flexibility, commitment, and rapidity of management decision-taking.

However one approaches the problem, and however logical a particular approach may appear to be – for example the appointment of an 'integrator' to piece together the contributions of different departments – it does seem difficult in this area to lay down hard-and-fast rules. Thus Burns and Shanks stress the need for flexibility, but presumably this leaves a good deal of discretion to individual managements to determine the exact nature of organisational arrangements. Those managements who favour a more structured approach may be open to criticism on the grounds of failure to give adequate scope for individual initiative, but at the same time will benefit from the advantages of formal planning mentioned earlier. In any case, where such an approach is found to 'work' in the particular in-house and market situation faced by a firm, it is difficult to argue that it should be changed, particularly in the absence of any evidence that any one approach is 'ideal' in all circumstances.

It is not intended to end this chapter on an uncertain note. On the other hand, an examination of organisational literature does suggest a rich variety of attack by companies. Perhaps the safest conclusion to hold to is that awareness on the part of managements of the importance of adequate organisational arrangements is more important than attention to the minutiae of the arrangements themselves.

Chapter 7

The Generation and Evaluation of New-Product Ideas

INTRODUCTION

We now depart from our pre-occupation with the evolutionary cycle of new products and its organisation to a more detailed examination of some of the major stages of new-product development, examining the process from the point of idea origination through to the market launch of the ultimate product. It may be useful to commence the chapter with a recent quotation.

> I want to insist, however, that technological change has been the mainspring of economic and social progress over the past two centuries, and that it remains the chief source of our increasing affluence. Whatever may be said to pooh-pooh or deride economic growth no-one would want us to go back to the mode of living of 1770, still less to the lower standards to which the present population would be reduced if we abandoned every improvement in technology since then. If one looks back, it is the introduction of new products and new techniques that increasingly dominates the process of growth.[1]

Statements of this sort are a reminder of the importance of new products to the economic well-being and standards of living of entire countries. Of obvious importance, too, is the need for individual firms to think creatively about new-product ideas in order to contribute to economic growth and to their own continuing profitability.

The way in which companies search for and evaluate new-product ideas is the concern of this chapter. In the light of the Cairncross statement, attempts to illuminate the process of idea generation within individual companies, or groups of companies (as is the present concern) should be given a high priority, particularly if improvements can be suggested.

CREATIVITY IN THE R AND D LABORATORY

The problems of R and D management command an extensive literature, much of which is beyond the scope of this study.[2] On the other hand, the present chapter necessarily impinges on some aspects of the conduct of R and D work in industry. Of particular importance are any factors constraining creative thinking about new products.

One major factor which will be mentioned here is organisational in character. The point which ought to be brought out is that the special activities involved in creative R and D work do not fit easily into the organisational structures set up for the conduct of other functional activities. This was emphasised in a recent work concerned with innovation:

> In both industry and government, a costly and dangerous trend is emerging, a trend towards a kind of management system whose pattern of operation is incompatible with that required for highly creative performance by scientific and engineering people. It is a trend towards tighter budgetary controls and tighter organisation of the work.[3]

As companies grow in size they tend to bring with them impersonal management and large-scale organisation, precisely the kinds of factors most likely to inhibit the creative individual inventor. Indeed it is not too much to suggest that good, creative personnel will thrive best in conditions of near anarchy, and the less constraint that is applied, without an actual descent to anarchy, the better will be the creativity.

This point is emphasised by Casimir. He urges that in employing scientists for creative laboratory work, little attention should be paid to the details of their previous experience, they should have much freedom, and their idiosyncrasies should be accepted. He also urges a middle course between individualism and strict regimentation, and advises 'in case of doubt favour anarchy'. Among his other proposals are that research laboratories should have independence in their choice of subject, and not be accountable to a detailed budget system.[4]

If such views are accepted it is clear that the more bureaucratic the organisation and regimentation that is aplied to the R and D facility, the lower will be the quality of its output. It is true that modern management principles and practices have an important part to play in large manufacturing and trading organisations. Applied to R and D, however, the result may be to reduce drastically individual initiative and creativity. The problems of R and D may therefore call for the use or organisational structures far different from those in use elsewhere in the firm. In particular there appears to be a strong case for organisation around small self-contained units set up to fulfil specific research ends.

The reader will not fail to note the similarity of the above argument to the points put forward by Burns (and also by Burns and Stalker) referred to at the end of the last chapter.[5] These authors, it will be recalled, urged the view that the task of organising industrial science was merely a matter of facilitating technical entrepreneuship. In other words, innovation is most likely to flourish in the more fluid organic company structure than in the more stratified mechanistic one. The freedom which Casimir wants creative scientists to have is clearly going to be found most readily in the former situation.

IDEA GENERATION BY NON R AND D PERSONNEL

The discussion to this point has focused on the contribution of creative R and D workers. This is obviously an unnecessary restriction given that various other members of a company can be encouraged to think along new lines. Personnel in direct contact with customers, for example field salesmen, seem particularly good potential idea sources.

Attractive though the proposal is that the new-ideas net

should be cast widely within the firm, such a procedure is not likely to function effectively without top management encouragement and support. Before turning to a consideration of individual idea sources, it is intended to summarise four main ways in which this support may be given.

Establishment of an adequate communications system

If new-product suggestions are to be sought widely within the firm, a communications system must be established to encourage the transmission of ideas from originators to senior management. The latter needs to ensure that such systems do not run into difficulties which may defeat their original purpose.

For example, the chief executive may let it be known widely within the firm that he is willing, even anxious, to discuss new-product suggestions conceived by individual employees on a face-to-face basis, but this may run counter to the lower-echelon employee's habit of communicating through the command hierarchy, that is his first inclination may be to report to the departmental head, who in turn may block the idea. In any case, lower-level employees may be reluctant to incur the disfavour of their immediate managers by bypassing them.

Karger and Murdick[6] stress the need for what they call an 'idea solicitor' whose function would be the systematic solicitation of ideas from technical, marketing and manufacturing personnel. However, they stress that few have the necessary knowledge and training to perform the task. Such an individual would require at least the following:

(1) an adequate technical and business background;
(2) an ability to command the confidence of others;
(3) an ability to act as a catalyst on many occasions; and
(4) a willingness to encourage 'free-wheeling' thoughts by new idea contributors.

Karger and Murdick go on to stress the dangers facing the solicitor of 'drying up' idea sources even if these are only mildly discouraged. While he may operate as the focal point of the communications system, it is clear that the system requires to be handled with delicacy.

Giving encouragement to idea proposers

The importance of encouraging company personnel to think about new ideas has already been implied in the above section. However, it should be added that casting a wide net for new-product ideas in a firm runs into the obstacle that many company employees will lack sufficient interest or motivation to concern themselves with new ideas. In some companies, managements' attempts to interest personnel in such areas as customer problems, product applications and new-product ideas, sometimes fall on stony ground, despite a laudable ambition to get staff more personally involved with company affairs. Nor need one look for an explanation of this lack of interest. For some employees the absence of additional remuneration, and the fact that 'extra' activity may take place outside normal working hours, are sufficient deterrents.

In this sense the stimulation of employee interest in new-idea generation is merely part of the management's general problem of employee motivation. However, as far as new-product ideas are concerned Karger and Murdick[7] suggest that specific questions can be drawn up and put to a wide variety of company personnel, with the prospect of good results if administered satisfactorily by the ideas solicitor. Examples of such questions are:

(1) What products can they see as a real need that the industry should develop and offer for sale?

(2) What new equipment, gadget, or mechanism would they like to see developed to help them in their work?

(3) What safety device is needed?

(4) What have they heard others say was needed as a new product?

The foregoing should not be taken to imply an absence of motivation on the part of many employees, for example sales personnel, R and D staff, and market researchers. Indeed such categories may make strenuous independent efforts to propose newer ideas. However, even in the upper echelons of management where a high degree of interest and motivation is to be expected, the pressures of day-to-day functional activities on departmental heads may hinder their full participation in idea generation.

Keeping the idea proposer informed

Successful operation of a new-product ideas programme in a firm requires not only that potential sources be encouraged, but also that those who have made proposals are kept informed of the progress of their ideas. The reasoning behind this statement is that the idea originator will tend to become discouraged if his idea merely 'disappears' into top management's administrative structure. Ideally the proposer should be advised if and when the idea is taken further and it may even be advisable to involve him in any committee activity set up to discuss it. Certainly, should the idea ultimately become a commercial reality, the firm's management will wish to think of various ways of according recognition to the proposer's contribution, ranging from financial reward to promotion to a post concerned with the manufacture and sale of the product.

Giving clear guidelines for creative thinking

While there are strong arguments in favour of encouraging free-ranging thought about new-product ideas, there is a case for disseminating in the firm some notion of product policies and customer requirements so that ideas will be stimulated in accord with the broad path the firm wishes to follow. Some firms find that unless these 'boundaries' are made explicit, individuals will form their own ideas, with the result that many ideas bear little relation to the company's needs. For example, one firm known to the authors making large-scale air-conditioning plant for industrial applications, has frequently been urged by internal staff to enter the domestic air-conditioning market. The suggestion continues to be rejected because of the firm's intention to remain specialists in the capital-goods sphere. However, this intention is not a matter of general company knowledge. Perhaps a more fruitful flow of ideas would be stimulated if over-all product and market objectives were made a matter of wider interest.

Marketing and management literature suggest methods for

channelling new product thinking along lines appropriate to the company's interest and capabilities. One such proposal is that of Ward.[8] Basically he suggests that an inventory of resources and skills should be drawn up and aggregated under three major headings. These would then take the form of three columns (Table 7.1 is an example). The first column contains details of the company's products, both present and past, and any under active consideration for the future. The second column details all processes, engineering skills and company capabilities including, for example, complex fabrication, hydraulics, and soil mechanics. A third column lists outlets.

TABLE 7.1   *Characteristic table*

PRODUCTS	PROCESSES	OUTLETS
Pumps	Dewatering	Domestic consumers
Air compressors	Crystallisation	Hardware shops
Thermal driers	Control engineering	Department stores
Centrifuges	Hydraulics	Motor manufacturers
Finned tubing	Pneumatics	Garages
Evaporators	Combustion	Chemical concerns
Pressure vessels	Heat balance	Construction companies
Refrigerators	Rotation	Plant-hire firms
Filters	Reciprocation	Builders' merchants
Lightweight diesels	Structures	Tonnage oxygen plants
Domestic heaters	Soil mechanics	Mining
Window fasteners	—	Docks
Air-conditioning	Extrusion	Electricity undertakings
Winches	Deep drawing	Aircraft industry
Escalators	Copy-turning	Research establishments
Cartridges	Broaching	Food-processing
Dish-washers	Chemical milling	Sewage and water boards
Car bumpers	Complex fabrication	Education authorities
Heated towel rails	Precision casting	The Services
Immersion heaters	Powder metallurgy	Hotels

Source: Ward, *The Dynamics of Planning.*

Ward then proposes a brain-storming technique within the parameters of the company 'profile' as laid down in the columns. In this way it is hoped that new-product suggestions, if at times bearing only a tenuous relationship with capabilities, will be stimulated. One approach is to examine the factors for any previously unnoticed, or underestimated, relationships. Thus products might include air compressors and air-conditioning equipment; experience might include pneumatics and supply of equipment for tonnage oxygen plants. The common link between these four items might suggest the broad area 'air handling and processing' which embraces, in addition, air conveying, air cleaning, air filtration and pressure exchangers. A new-products search directed along these and similar lines is more likely to yield ideas compatible with the firm's capabilities and objectives than a very broadly based search.

SELECTED INTERNAL SOURCES

Having discussed some of the problems facing managements in creating a favourable climate for the encouragement of new ideas in the firm, it will now be appropriate to consider selected sources with comments on their usefulness.

Technological Forecasting

The importance of this activity in helping the firm to achieve a balanced use of its resources in the light of current and emerging market requirements was dwelled on in Chapter 4. It is now intended to say something of the importance of this activity in suggesting new-product ideas.

Foster[9] takes the view that if planning for new products and markets is to be successful, executives 'cannot avoid' undertaking technological forecasting, which he defines as forecasting how technology relevant and peripheral to their business is likely to change over the period of the corporate long-range plans and beyond. Taking the problem of pollution in a country as an example, he notes that this forecasting will look at the possibilities of new methods (for controlling pollution) becoming available which would operate at acceptable costs, and at other technical developments which will overcome the problem of cost.

However, Foster stresses certain limitations of technological forecasting. One of these is the possibility of major discoveries and breakthroughs occurring, perhaps without warning, for example xerography which has displaced former methods of duplication in many areas. In other words, technological forecasting cannot predict everything, but Foster notes that the close interdependence between technological forecasting and the planning of the firm's future is now recognised by executives.

Market Research

Whereas technological forecasting is concerned with likely changes in technology in the future, and the implications of these changes for new products, conventional market research can be given the perhaps less daunting, but still demanding, task of seeking new-product possibilities available on a licensing basis or other agreement. The objective of a company may be to seek out a substantial list of products in a particular area of interest, for example the leisure market, domestic heating, and so forth, with a view to possible manufacture under licence, or perhaps independent development.

Such a search, if done thoroughly, calls for an exhaustive exploration of numerous research publications, as well as direct contact with licence and patent agents, and various bodies which will be outlined in more detail in the next section (dealing with external sources of information). However, the market-research team will wish, in addition, to attend relevant conferences and exhibitions and perhaps directly approach manufacturing concerns. The objective of such a comprehensive search is to ensure that no important opportunities are overlooked, so that a high probability exists of finding worthwhile opportunities.

Searching of this sort may be performed by the in-house market-research department, or by specialist consultants, and either as a 'one-off' search or as a continuing activity. There are attractions in the last-named approach in that the company will seek to inform itself on an on-going basis of all new-product opportunities emerging in its chosen fields of interest.

Sales and Service Personnel

Such individuals tend to have a narrow view conditioned by existing products, and because of the nature of their activities may be unable to take an objective viewpoint. It can be argued that sales personnel are *by definition* non-objective and, as such, are not fruitful idea sources. Their lack of objectivity also makes them suspect as market researchers, though some companies employ them in this role. There is a need for management to think again about the wisdom of asking sales personnel to perform non-selling functions without corresponding changes in training and job descriptions.

Senior Management

Distinct dangers exist in being over-dependent on this source. It is true that senior management, in part because of top-level contact with users and others, can suggest ideas not available to others in the firm. On the other hand, the simple fact of the seniority of such executives can on occasion lead to the pursuit of dubious projects.

In one case known to the authors, a firm's basic motivation for entering the road-tanker market was that the Chairman had been impressed by the apparent healthy state of the market for these vehicles overseas and in effect directed the company to enter the field. In another case, a senior technical director whose 'brainchild' a new-product idea was, took upon himself the role of sponsor, and was apparently willing to suppress adverse information about technical-development snags.

However, to be completely impartial, there is plenty of evidence indicating a growing willingness among senior management to take cognisance of disinterested technical and market research.

SELECTED EXTERNAL SOURCES

While company functions such as sales and market research have been described as internal sources of new-product ideas, clearly a major input of information they will provide is derived from areas external to the firm in the shape of customers, competitors, and so on. It is to a consideration of these external sources that we now turn.

Karger and Murdick[10] list a number of idea sources which derive from outside the firm and it may be useful to highlight the major areas they describe.

Solicited and unsolicited ideas

In this case Karger and Murdick suggest the possibility of the firm actively soliciting ideas from outside sources, for example research laboratories and other companies. However, they recommend great care in using this approach because of the danger of being 'swamped' by numerous ideas, many of which are 'stale'. Another danger is that the discloser may not provide adequate information on the availability of patent protection. If the patent has expired, or is not owned by the discloser, then obvious dangers of patent infringement exist for the firm if it chooses to pursue the idea.

Many companies will receive unsolicited ideas, perhaps from independent inventors, though this cannot be regarded as a major contemporary source of new-product ideas. On the other hand, it should be stressed that freelance inventors are still credited with some important product innovations, and Hill *et al.*[11] remind us that C. F. Carlson's copying machine and Edwin Land's camera were both rejected by blue-chip companies, forcing the men to form their own enterprises – Xerox and Polaroid.

Other Companies

It may prove useful to examine other companies who have patented products outside the area of their normal interests. Companies holding such unused patents may be quite willing to license others to use them.

Licences granted by one manufacturer to another usually involve an initial payment plus a subsequent royalty on sales, the initial payment being designed to cover the transfer of knowhow, drawings, and so on.

That other companies may be a fruitful idea source is reinforced by the consideration that, for the licensor, certain advantages of granting a licence exist. Among these Ward[12] cites the following:

(1) it brings additional income without additional capital outlay, factory space, plant or personnel;

(2) the risk is comparatively slight, effectively an opportunity risk in that some other course may have yielded more return;

(3) a licensee, unlike an agent, will have interests closely coinciding with those of the licensor;

(4) the licensee has a sales force on the spot and a knowledge of local conditions; and

(5) customers usually prefer a home product or a product supplied by a local manufacturer.

Research Laboratories

Karger and Murdick point to the importance of industrial-research laboratories as idea sources and note that these will develop products on a contract basis for client companies, or will offer ideas on a licence basis.

Basically the searching company needs to be aware of what organisations exist throughout the world, and what they can offer in terms of new-product possibilities. Such organisations include sponsored research establishments such as the Illinois Institute of Technology and Battelle Memorial Institute and national bodies such as the United Kingdom Atomic Energy Authority and the National Engineering Laboratory. Moreover, one should include here the educational institutions in a country providing degrees in engineering and/or science which must be considered potential idea sources.

In so far as organisations such as these work on a contract basis, it is possible to approach them with a request to seek and/or develop new products. The reasons for utilising these services are quite numerous, and include the following:[13]

(1) the firm's engineering or research staff is loaded and cannot accept additional work without expansion;

(2) the existing engineering and/or research skills in the company may not be well suited to the desired product;

(3) the laboratory or institute has the required specialised personnel and / or facilities; and

(4) the company desires to see the results from scientists who are not as rigidly controlled within the company.

Middlemen

By this term Karger and Murdick mean established intermediaries with new-product interests. These will be distributed throughout the world, and as Ward notes[14] includes patent agents, licence brokers, product consultants, merchant banks, commercial attachés and licensing organisations in communist and socialist countries, including Licensintor (the Soviet Union), Polytechna (Czechoslovakia), Polservice (Poland) and Nikex (Hungary).

Outside individuals

Categories such as military personnel, civilians working on military projects, and company personnel working for competing companies, can in theory be approached for ideas, but the limitations are obvious, perhaps most notably the moral obligation of such people not to disclose confidential information.

Ideas from abroad

Although Karger and Murdick put this forward as a separate category, clearly the conscientious firm contacting sources such as the research establishments and middlemen described above, will already be thinking in international terms.

However, there is merit in bringing to one's search a strong awareness of the possible differences between one's home market and those overseas, and the implications of these differences for new product ideas.

Taking U.S. companies as an example, Karger and Murdick point to three types of items existing in Europe which sometimes fit into their domestic marketing programmes:

(1) products on the European market, which are successful

in that market, but which have never been introduced in the United States;

(2) products never successful in Europe due to the conditions in that market, but which could succeed in the United States; and

(3) products being developed in European laboratories which might be successful in the United States when complete.

Printed and published sources of ideas

There are numerous sources of published information concerned with new-product ideas and literature searches in relevant periodicals, and other current published information can be carried out in parallel with solicitation of ideas from other sources. In this way the coverage should be comprehensive.

Since the number of sources is so great, and vary from time to time, it is intended to show a brief list of journals devoted to new products, or with new-product sections appearing in them. Table 7.2 offers such a list.

TABLE 7.2 *New-product journals*

Clipper Cargo Horizons Pan American World Airways Inc., Pan Am Building, New York, N.Y. 10017, U.S.A.	Lists worldwide marketing and licensing opportunities
Engineering 36 Bedford Street, London, WC2	Illustrated paragraphs on new engineering products under 'Engineering ways and means'
Industrial Bulletin 450 Ohio Street, Chicago 11, Illinois, U.S.A.	
Industrial Equipment News Tothill Press Limited, 161 Fleet Street, London, EC4	Details of new American industrial products
International Licensing Pinner, Middlesex	Lists worldwide licences offered

Inventions and Designs Licensed to Industry
United Kingdom Atomic Energy Authority,
11 Charles ii Street,
London, SW1

Inventions for Industry
National Research Development Corporation,
Kingsgate House,   Details of new inventions under
66–74 Victoria Street,   subject heading – mainly British
London, SW1   patents

New Equipment Digest
Penton Building,
Cleveland,
Ohio, U.S.A.

New Product Newsletter
135 E. 44th Street,
New York,
N.Y. 10017, U.S.A.   Worldwide details of new products

Newsweek
Kinbex House,   Page devoted each week to new
Wellington Street,   products, both consumer and
Slough, Bucks   industrial

New Technology
42 Parliament Street,   Prepared by Ministry of Technology
London, SW1   and the Central Office of Information

Patent Abstract Series
Office of Technical Services,
Washington 25, D.C.,
U.S.A.

Product Licensing Index
Industrial Opportunities Limited,
13–14 Homewell,
Havant, Hants   Worldwide licences available

Production Equipment Digest
Hulton Publications Limited,
55 Saffron House,
London, EC1   New British products

Products List Circular
Small Business Administration,
Washington 25, D.C.,
U.S.A.   Details of American patents

Soviet Technology Bulletin
CIS Limited,
6 Greenway Park,
Galmpton,   New methods and products from
Brixham, Devon   Soviet articles

Technical Digest
Spalena 51,   Translations of socialist countries'
Prague 1,   magazines and details of new
Czechoslovakia   products and processes

Source: Ward, *The Dynamics of Planning*, p. 131.

Competitors

Although Karger and Murdick do not accord this source a separate heading, we feel it should be mentioned specifically.

Most companies are probably aware of the need to take account of competitor activity, though the thoroughness with which this is done will vary from firm to firm. In some cases, competitor company reports and accounts will be regularly examined for profitability data, technical literature and trade press for designs used, and there will be constant reporting by sales personnel on other activities of rival firms. There is clearly a widespread and understandable desire on the part of most companies not to be outdistanced by rivals.

However, this source may not be a significant one in terms of new-product ideas involving new technologies. This is partly because R and D personnel in general often believe they know from which direction the next technological breakthrough will come, and they believe this knowledge is widely shared. The ability of the major computer manufacturers to keep pace relatively quickly with the new technologies associated with the successive generations of these machines (for example valve, transistor, micro-integrated circuitry) bears testimony to this.[15]

SCREENING AND EVALUATING NEW-PRODUCT IDEAS

The company performing the search activities described above will necessarily generate numerous ideas. These, in turn, will require to be assessed by management for their suitability. It is to the problems of idea evaluation that we now turn.

A study of empirical evidence suggests that companies, when evaluating new-product proposals, attach importance to qualitative judgements and subjective factors rather than the use of strictly quantified procedures. For example, Williams[16] found, in a study of thirteen firms, that for many projects prospective yields were not calculated, and where they were, they were often crude. Variety in method was typical, and small use was made of such techniques as discounted cash flow. Again, Olin's[17] survey concluded that in the European chemical

THE GENERATION AND EVALUATION OF NEW-PRODUCT IDEAS 111

industry, project selection remains 'a pragmatic and intuitive art'. This situation reflects the very considerable technical and market uncertainties involved in product innovation.

A partial alternative to a quantified cost–benefit or D.C.F. approach is to use a qualitative checklist method of evaluation. Such an approach has the advantage of being able to take into account many factors which may defy incorporation in a mathematical formula. It may be useful to look briefly at three such factors, which have been noted by Freeman.[18] These are:

(1) The enthusiasm and capacity of the project leader. This is a critical factor in the success of any R and D project. The leader's other commitments need to be considered also.

(2) The firm's resources of skilled people and accumulated knowhow in the field and the possible spin-off from other R and D projects.

(3) The firm's relationship with customers.

Freeman notes that while all these factors may be taken into account by a research manager or an entrepreneur in calculating probability factors for technical or commercial success, a checklist procedure has the merit of compelling systematic attention to be made to each point.

It will be useful at this point to dilate upon the matter of screening and provide an example of a screening list.

Practical approaches to idea screening

Basically, idea screening calls for an explicit listing of criteria to be used in the judgement of new-product proposals. It is in essence an information-seeking and appraisal process in which the information sought is not only on the characteristics of a product but also on these relative to certain external factors. The object of the process is not to determine in absolute terms whether a proposed product should be added to a company's product-mix, rather it is to indicate whether further detailed investigation is justified.

One formal qualitative screening process is that described by Wilson.[19] It may be useful to outline its major elements to provide some insight into the rationale of the procedure. Table 7.3 sets out the actual screening list used.

TABLE 7.3 *Qualitative screening process**

PRODUCT........

A Section	B Coding	C Factor	D Weighting	E Rating	F Score
POSITION	a	Ease of development of manufacturing process	2	+2	+4
	b	Value added by in-company processing	1	0	0
	c	Exclusive or favoured purchasing position	1	+2	+2
	d	Effect on purchasing position	1	0	0
	e	Availability of raw materials within company	2	−2	−4
	f	Effect on negotiating position	1	+1	+1
R and D	a	Utilisation of existing knowhow	1	0	0
	b	Relationship to future development planning	2	−2	−4
	c	Utilisation of existing laboratory or pilot plant equipment	1	+1	+1
	d	Availability of R and D personnel	1	+2	+2
ENGINEERING	a	Reliability of process or knowhow	2	−1	−2
	b	Utilisation of standardised equipment	1	+2	+2
	c	Availability of engineering personnel	2	+2	+4
STABILITY	a	Durability of the market	3	+1	+3
	b	Breadth of the market	2	−1	−2
	c	Possibility of captive market	1	−2	−2
	d	Difficulty in copying	1	−2	−2
	e	Stability in depressions	2	+1	+2
	f	Stability in wartime	1	+1	+1

			Weighting	Rating	Weighted rating
GROWTH	a	Unique character of product or process	2	−2	−4
	b	Demand-supply ratio	3	0	0
	c	Ratio of technical change	1	+2	+2
	d	Export possibilities	1	−2	−2
	e	Improved opportunities for management personnel	2	+2	+4
MARKETABILITY	a	Relationship to existing markets	2	+1	+2
	b	Company's image in allied fields	1	+2	+2
	c	Ease of market penetration	1	−2	−2
	d	Company's ability to give technical service requirements	2	−1	−2
	e	Competition with customer's products	2	+2	+4
	f	User stratification	1	+1	+1
	g	Few variations required	1	+1	+1
	h	Freedom from seasonal fluctuations	2	−1	−2
PRODUCTION	a	Utilisation of idle equipment	1	−2	−2
	b	Utilisation of surplus steam, electricity and water	1	+2	+2
	c	Utilisation and upgrading of by-products	1	−2	−2
	d	Utilisation of process familiar to company personnel	1	0	0
	e	Availability of production and maintenance workers	2	+2	+4
	f	Plant maintenance requirements	1	0	0
	g	Ability to cope with waste disposal problems	1	+2	+2
	h	Ability to cope with hazardous operating conditions	1	+2	+2

Over-all weighted rating (score)   + 16
Maximum weighted rating (score)   +116
Minimum weighted rating (score)   −116

* The weighting, rating and scores in this table are for an imaginary product: 'Bituminous materials for spreading composition'.

Wilson's proposed method of screening has four phases:

(1) the preparation of an inventory of the company's resources;[20]

(2) the preparation and use of the first coarse screen in which obvious deterrents to the development and marketing of the product are identified;

(3) the preparation of the fine screen (see Table 7.3) which comprises a series of questions to which answers for decision-taking need to be obtained; and

(4) the rating of the product in relation to each of the elements of the fine screen and the weighting of the questions relatively to each other.

The audit of total company resources is regarded as the first phase of the screening process, and as was noted in Chapter 4 its purpose is to produce some assessment of company strengths and weaknesses. The relevance of the audit to screening is that at the final stage of this process, the over-all characteristics of a product can be judged against the resources already present within the company.

The second phase is concerned with the identification and evaluation of obvious deterrents: 'factors which, if negative, would be sufficient on their own to warrant discontinuation of, not only the screening process, but any further activities within the firm relating to the product's development'.[21] This stage is therefore concerned with glaring arguments for discontinuation, for example the impossibility of obtaining patents or extreme difficulty in obtaining relevant raw-material supplies. Some product ideas therefore inevitably disappear at this coarse-screening stage but those remaining require more detailed study.

The third phase involves preparation of the fine screen by means of which relevant questions are listed. The answers to these are intended to provide an assessment of, for example, market stability and growth, and the R and D, production and marketing requirements of the new product. For convenience it is useful to place associated questions in groups, for example growth, stability and position. These groupings are then integrated into a table of possibly thirty to forty questions.

Stage four is concerned with evaluating new products

against the fine-screening factors. Methods of performing this task have been progressively improved in recent years, culminating in the development of computerised techniques for dealing with the appropriate calculations.[22] One method (see Table 7.3) is to rate each product against each factor:

+2 very good
+1 good
 0 average
−1 poor
−2 very poor

Weighting of factors can be accomplished by using a simple semantic scale:

3 essential
2 preferable
1 interesting
0 irrelevant

A product's score needs to reflect not only the answers to each question, but also the relative importance of the questions. Its score in relation to each question is therefore obtained by multiplying the weighted value by the rated value, the scores for all the questions being added to give the product's over-all score. (Table 7.3 gives a worked example.)

It is not our intention (nor indeed is it that of Wilson) to lay down rigid methods for screening new products. Our purpose has been to indicate the type of process that may usefully be adopted by a firm. However, if screens of this type are used, their elements may require to be varied from time to time to suit changing company and market circumstances. Certainly, as Freeman[23] stresses, more far-sighted firms may also want to take into account additional external costs and benefits, such as problems of waste disposal or employment effects, retraining requirements and contributions to research outside the company.

It is as well to stress, however, that despite its advantages, screening procedures do suffer certain serious limitations. For example, they do not permit easy comparison between alternative projects, nor do they provide any indication of the likely absolute size of the pay-off. As most firms have a backlog of candidate projects from which to select, these must be regarded as major drawbacks. In consequence, it will be necessary to think in terms of augmenting screening procedures to take such problems into account, and this problem is considered below.

Towards an ideal screening procedure

Freeman contends that the ideal method of project selection is probably a combination of a quantitative cost–benefit approach with a qualitative checklist approach. Several such 'scoring systems' have been developed, and Freeman illustrates that originally worked out for project evaluation at Morganite by Hart.[24] (See Figure 7.1)

Basically Hart's system involves calculation of a project index value, which takes account of estimated peak-sales value, net profit on sales, probability of R and D technical success and a time discount factor in relation to future R and D costs according to the formula:

$$I \text{ (index value)} = \frac{S \times P \times p \times t}{100\ C}$$

where S = peak sales value £ per annum, P = net profit on sales (per cent), p = probability of R and D success on a scale 0 to 1, t = a time discount factor, and C = future cost of R and D (£).

As Freeman notes, estimates for the variables are obtained by answering a checklist of questions. Figure 7.1 shows a score for each possible answer to the question and permits scoring by addition rather than multiplication by using logarithmic functions of the answers. The method can be varied by using different questions and different scores to suit the circumstances of a particular firm.

In Freeman's view, the system offers two major advantages:

(1) It permits consideration of such factors as external competition and customer attitudes, yet at the same time ranks projects on some systematic basis, on the assumption of sales growth and high profitability as major company objectives; and

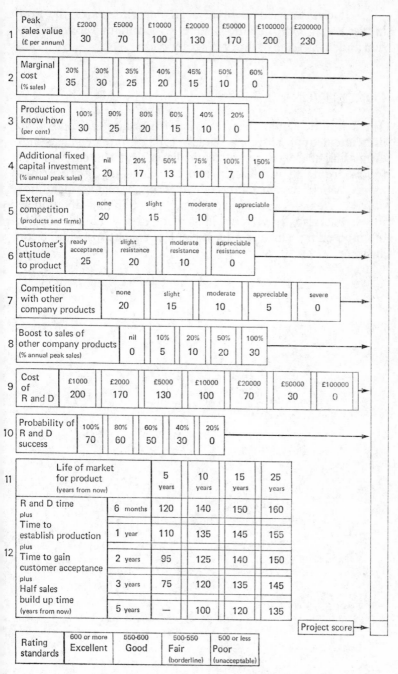

FIG. 7.1 *Evaluation chart for product and projects*

(2) It can be used to involve all departments of the firm in discussion and evaluation, thereby contributing to mobilisation and integration of the firm's resources.

CONCLUSION

There is little doubt that much advice awaits the innovative firm intent upon searching widely for new-product ideas and evaluating these on a systematic basis. But success will not follow from the installation and carrying out of procedures alone. Much responsibility devolves upon management not only to create a propitious climate for thinking about new ideas, but also to exercise judgement about the desirability of proceeding when static formulae cannot provide clear answers.

Chapter 8

New-Product Design and Technical Development

INTRODUCTION

The company, proceeding in the logical manner we have suggested, will ultimately come to the point of deciding whether or not to go ahead with a new idea. At the culmination of screening and more detailed financial evaluation the hope is that some candidate products will stand out most clearly as potential 'winners'. The cautious firm will not commit itself immediately and may feel that a further period of detailed market research is necessary before making a final decision. Also, it is as well to repeat that the firm may keep its eyes open to merger or acquisition possibilities as an entrée to the market. However, in this chapter we will assume a decision is made to proceed by internal design and technical development.

Let us commence by stressing the importance of market information as an input to the design process. Thus Asimow states that

> The starting point of a design project is a hypothetical need which may have been observed currently on the socioeconomic scene. It may be phrased in the form of a primitive statement resting on untested observations; or it may have been elaborated into a sophisticated and authenticated statement based on market and consumer studies.[1]

The value of marketing's contribution to the design of a wide range of manufactured products has also been emphasised in the Feilden Report.[2]

E

However, it is as well to sound a cautionary note and emphasise that even the most exhaustive and elaborate market research will not necessarily guarantee successful innovation. A case in point is the perhaps well-known one of Corfam. Du Pont's work in this area included the development of a computer model of the world market for hides, leather and shoes, and extensive field trials of thousands of pairs of shoes to ensure an acceptable, comfortable and hygienic design. Yet the venture failed, the company ultimately retiring the product from the market.

On the other hand, marketing literature is replete with examples of the way in which sophisticated market study has made indispensable contributions to new-product design. The Feilden Report suggests that poor designing has been a major factor in the United Kingdom's loss of exports in various industries, and goes on to suggest that the principal failing is a marketing one, namely a failure to ensure that customer requirements are fully understood and interpreted. Specification of what is wanted by the consumer is, in the words of this authoritative document, 'the key to design'.

The dilemma facing management is obvious enough – marketable designs may not be guaranteed by market research. Its absence does not necessarily spell failure. On the other hand, it is difficult to defend companies who cling to traditional designs when world market demand is moving towards greater sophistication. (Feilden roundly berates such firms, holding them in part responsible for the poor market performance of some industries abroad.)

Designing successfully for the needs of the market-place is a more complex business than is sometimes appreciated in the marketing literature. In particular there may be some tendency to play down the contribution of the individual designer working independently. This and additional problems are discussed below. It is suggested that statements concerning the contribution of marketing to design probably need to be phrased more guardedly than has come to be fashionable in some industries. Moreover, it is emphasised that managements will require to consider a variety of informational and creative inputs in addition to market research.

DESIGNING FOR THE NEEDS OF THE MARKET

Marketing literature is filled with statements that correct attitudes are more important than the possession of formal departments or the practice of formal techniques. As far as managements are concerned, it will be a matter of indifference whether a formal market-research department, in liaison with the design office, exists or not, so long as the end-result of marketable products is attained. Thus the firm deliberately directing resources to the design area, and controlled by a forward-looking management team, may be able to design very successfully for the market without further assistance.

Let us consider in more detail the difficulties which companies may face in pursuing marketable designs.

The Limitations of User Surveys

The Chairman of the Marketing Society stated recently that, 'We are only now beginning to recognise that we cannot simply ask people what they want then hope to design a product which is acceptable to the market as a whole.'[3] The speaker went on to make the point that in the case of the Edsel car consumer research was conducted extensively, the problem being that the eventual design incorporated so many compromises to satisfy variations in taste that in the end no one was satisfied. Increasingly the approach should be to design the product in the first instance, then to check if market appreciation of the idea is likely. The exhortation to 'do market research' before developing a new product is therefore too simple according to this speaker. Given that all competitors in a particular industry can conduct broadly similar market studies and produce broadly similar results, there is a growing need to reassess the contribution of the creative designer to product differentiation.

Willsmer's suggested approach to the use of market research in product design to some extent echoes the attitude of Ewing. Ewing takes the view that the persuasive and widely held notion that market studies should precede any company planning activity is not necessarily correct.[4] He provides examples from electronic engineering to show the successful growth of a company which rejected diversification as a strategy for growth and chose to concentrate on a relatively narrow line of products for which the competition was intense. In another example Ewing points out that the company, a furniture manufacturer, in deciding whether or not to launch a new style line, has 'bet consistently on the judgement of their own style designers. Only after an innovation is decided on do they begin thinking about how to sell it.'

Ewing refers to a 'kind of empirical marketing judgement' which appears to be built into the actions of such firms. In almost all cases he cites it would appear that company managements have used the firm's experience in the market-place to determine what the organisation is exceptionally good at, and then designed programmes to exploit the ability as the decisive element in planning. In this setting, Ewing sees the role of marketing as one of *checking* or *constraining* strategies conceived in a thought process that has begun *at some other point*.

The Nature of the Product

The value of formal market study as an input to design is to a large extent a function of the type of product under consideration. Let us, for illustrative purposes, take the case of a firm manufacturing instruments.[5] This company adopts a threefold division of projects and finds that the scope of market research varies between them. '*A*' projects are those destined for quantity production which will eventually go into the company's catalogues. In this instance market research in depth to determine commercial potential is regarded as essential. '*B*' projects are custom-built products, special contracts, or a short-order run for a customer or for market evaluation. Such designs normally originate in response to a specification submitted by the customer, or as a result of discussions between the technical staff of the company and that of the customer. Market research is limited in this case, as is sales participation, because the company wishes to avoid discussion by salesmen of the product with other customers. Finally, the company recognises a '*C*' category which is described as 'speculative', involving, for example, exploratory design studies. Market research is not regarded as being of much value and has even been found to be misleading. A major reason for this is that if designs are revolutionary they do not figure in the 'preference scales' of customers so that market research would be in difficulty. The company has experience of products which eventually became market leaders despite adverse comment by sales management. Thus, the company management feels it 'must be prepared to back the hunches of development staff if it is to break into new fields'.

The Usefulness of Market Opinion

Because market research is not a persuasive sales function, it cannot by itself induce customers to favour more simplified designs or, for that matter, any kind of design. It is for this reason that some companies introduce new designs based largely on the designer's ideas. The argument is that consumer preference is in any case a function of what is available on the market. A customer cannot express a desire for a new design unless he has been exposed to it.

This general point of view has been expressed by more than one writer. Asimow, for example, recognises that the design process can commence without a need being present at all. 'The need may not yet exist, but there may be evidence that it is latent, and that it can be evoked when economic means for its satisfaction become available. The need may be suggested by a technical accomplishment that makes the means of its satisfaction possible.'[6] Ewing also states that 'A company can create a market by what it does – at least, if it does the job well.'[7] Finally, Schon points out that, in the process of development, need and technology interact.[8] The market originally conceived for the product may be ruled out by technical limitations discovered in the process of invention. The product for which a market must be anticipated is not an 'it' that remains constant. The product changes, and the market with it. The market is in this sense a function of the product, but the nature of the function is never clear ahead of time and may remain unclear throughout the product's life.

Such arguments suggest that the successful introduction of

a new-product design is likely to be a more complex affair than the simple application of market-research techniques.

The Contribution of the Designer's Market Knowledge

Frequently, the reply 'the designer should know' is given to questions about the way in which companies seek to incorporate user needs, for example ergonomic and aesthetic factors, into designs. This apparent dependence on the designer rather than market research is unlikely to be greeted with much enthusiasm by marketing specialists.

On the other hand, designers do not see themselves plunging into immediate disaster. Broadbent, for example, who has contributed much to the development of design method, refers to 'those curious things, almost mystical to design methodologists, called "clients' needs" '.[9] He concedes that a great deal of what designers do is concerned with finding out what these needs are, and a design process can be built up to take them into account. But he points out that such a process has an inherent disadvantage, namely that the end-result may turn out to be 'very similar to what the designer believes he does in any case'.

Could it be that the marketing fraternity has too little faith in the independent ability of designers to make good marketing decisions, and too much faith in the ability of current market-research methods to solve design problems?

The Iterative Nature of the Design Process

An important characteristic of the design process, whether formalised or not, is its iterative nature. It does not occur in a simple sequential fashion. The designer's solution to the problem posed by market research may, when analysed, exceed or fail to meet market requirements. If so, the design objective may have to be changed, or the entire design process repeated with new concepts and further evaluation and comparison made with market needs. Again, it may become apparent that manufacturing or cost considerations demand a change. Such change must be appraised for its impact on the rest of the design and on the likely attainment of the objective.

The specification of market requirements by market research for use by the engineering designer might therefore be the consequence of not one but *several* trips to the marketplace. The first of these might consist of the marketing department offering a promise of a new product and illustrating the offer by an original scheme created by the engineering designer. As the design progresses repeated contact with the market may be called for.

At the prototype stage, for example, it will be necessary to check if the design fulfils the original objective. If not, it may be necessary to back-track to previous stages and the design concept may be altered. A new concept may arise which appears more likely to satisfy customer needs. This would require to be evaluated by quantitative analysis where possible (for example suitability to meet stress requirements) and by qualitative judgement (for example aesthetic appeal).

The iterative nature of the design process, in particular its influence on the design/market interface, complicates the task of producing worthwhile specifications of requirement from the market. This difficulty is apparently not always appreciated by those who advocate that designers should work solely from market-research briefs, implying a simple sequential flow from market to design.

PROBLEMS OF INTERNAL GENERATION OF DESIGNS

The foregoing has suggested that designing for the market may be a more involved process than is sometimes believed. This is not, however, an argument in favour of 'ivory-tower' designing. Indeed, the opposite is the case. There is a need for an increase in effort towards improving the sophistication of market-research techniques of all types. Thus Ewing argues that although companies should avoid over-dependence on market studies as a basis for company planning, market analyses have changed from a 'luxury' resource to a 'must' tool.[10] In particular, he stresses that no matter how much 'market-creating' ability a company may possess, it cannot go too far 'against the tide' as far as the market is concerned.

Tentative objectives conceived by design teams may be rejected for marketing reasons. In this connection the value of market study is seen in terms of checking or constraining policies conceived internally.

The absence of a strong marketing approach can be a major factor in leading some companies into difficulties. Some important problems are highlighted below.

Imitative Designing

Some companies apparently believe that marketable designs will flow from copying other products. A great deal of importance is sometimes attached to studying the features of successful imported products, and 'features lists' may be drawn up from import statistics. The features of competitive domestically produced products may also be examined.

This approach is based upon the assumption that the activities of competitors reflect the best assessment of market needs. This faith may not be justified, and independent market study might reveal major areas of unsatisfied customer need. The approach is, in addition, passive and likely to restrict design innovations. This passivity appears to afflict certain sections of U.K. industry according to the Feilden Report, it being stated that in cases such as marine engines, textile, and agricultural machinery, design innovations come mostly from abroad.

Danger of Poor Detail Designing

The Feilden Report states that a basic deficiency of engineering designs generally in the United Kingdom is a failure adequately to meet the practical requirements of users, that is a failure of *detail* design. A design concept may be brilliant – for example the attainment, in mechanical terms, of an imaginative solution to a problem posed by the marketing department where the customer cannot define his requirements precisely. The design may fail to win customer approval, however, because of poor detail.

Asimow provides a listing of detail-design factors.[11] Their purpose, he states, is to incorporate in the design 'adequate service features' and to provide a rational basis for product improvement and redesign. The factors enumerated are:

   (1) design for maintenance;
   (2) design for reliability;
   (3) design for safety;
   (4) design for convenience in use (taking account of human factors);
   (5) design for aesthetic features;
   (6) design for operational economy;
   (7) design for adequate duration of service; and
   (8) the procurement of service data that can provide a basis for product improvement, for next-generation designs, and for the design of different but related products.

The Feilden Report cites a number of instances of failure at the detail stage. 50 per cent of the total cost of the Royal Air Force is stated to be maintenance, and aircraft spares alone cost £100m. per annum. The major cause of this situation is seen as being a lack of designed-in reliability and maintainability, in other words an ignorance of usage conditions. Analysis of defects indicated few associated with the integrity of main aircraft structures.

User Detail-Design Priorities

The importance attached to different combinations of detail-design factors varies between customers, industries and market segments, as well as through time. Government buyers may be less concerned with price than with quality. On the other hand, price may dominate where technical obsolescence is rapid and the economic working life of products is short or where customers have become more cost-conscious. This might require the application of value analysis or value engineering techniques in the design of the product to reduce its costs and so its price. Reliability is important when a high-quality job is needed by the buyer's customers, for example supplying equipment to boilermakers working on nuclear contracts. Ease of training is important if skilled labour is difficult to obtain in an industry. Labour saving is important if the cost of labour increases relative to the cost of capital.

Although the designer may satisfactorily design to suit the economic, ergonomic and other requirements of existing users, he is unlikely in the absence of market information to have knowledge of the *trend* in the importance of, say, after-sales service in a particular market segment, or indeed in the market as a whole. In this sense the designer needs to collaborate closely with marketing staff. Such is the importance of such co-ordination that it is intended to dwell on the matter at greater length in the next section.

THE IMPORTANCE OF DESIGN MARKETING CO-ORDINATION

One way to summarise the foregoing discussion would be to say that the company's approach to product design can vary between two extremes. On the one hand, the creative designer may be given free rein, with benefits accruing from his free-ranging creativity, but with the disadvantage that vital aspects of market requirements are ignored. On the other hand, the designer may be asked to work solely on the basis of market-research briefs prepared by the marketing department, with the advantage that work is deliberately geared towards the market, but with the danger that design creativity and individuality is impaired. Many firms will, however, favour a middle course, seeking to inform themselves through market study about market attitudes to design, while simultaneously encouraging creative thinking on the part of the design staff.

Whatever approach is used, few would dispute the need to seek the greatest co-ordination of the work of various individuals whose activities can, and should, influence design. There are grounds for believing that the design effort in many companies lacks a formality of organisation which would enable the (possibly conflicting) views of all relevant parties to be considered. The views of the sales and service organisation and those obtained via market research are of particular significance. The sales force may not be fully consulted on design matters, and market research in the sense of formal surveys may often be absent. The design engineer may be a law unto himself, although this is not a necessary prescription for failure.

There is therefore a persuasive case for utilising the relevant contributions of market research while taking sales and design opinion into account. Not all firms operate a design process capable of absorbing these different viewpoints. The authors have, however, recently studied the integrated approach of a successful machine-tool firm which took the view that the best results could only be obtained by a pooling of resources and opinions.[12] A summary of the approach is given below. The reader should note, however, the sequence of events favoured.

Case Study of Co-ordinated Design Approach

The design process in this company's case commences with a formal market survey, conducted by trained market researchers, to attempt to ascertain the size of the market for the proposed new machine and an estimate of sales likely to be achieved. The resulting report – referred to as a marketing brief – is submitted for Board discussion. If approval for further work is forthcoming, the next stage is an advanced design survey conducted by trained market-research engineers to determine product specifications. (The company has now built up a library of such reports.)

The next stage involves the sales force. Sales personnel are asked to comment on the specifications, and as a result of these deliberations design proposals are refined and modified by design staff. At this stage various functions become involved, including production, maintenance and value engineering to consider manufacturing and other problems of the new design. Value engineering is of particular significance where there are difficulties in meeting the likely market price. At the end of this period of joint activity, the design specification is ratified and reference is again made to the sales department to check if any factors influencing product saleability have appeared. If no major obstacles are reported, the design moves to the prototype building stage.

There can be no certainty, however, that success will automatically result from following such an approach, if one considers that successful design innovations continue to be initiated using less-formalised procedures. Also, it still remains true that market research possesses 'blind spots', for example where buyers cannot define in detail what they require. Further, while sales opinion is of value, it too has limitations, particularly where the salesman is asked to perform quasi-market-research functions without specific training.

TECHNICAL DEVELOPMENT

Following logically from the design process discussed above is that of technical development aimed at producing a working model or prototype of the new product.

Clearly this is a stage of intense technical/engineering activity, and discussion of such problems is beyond the scope of this book. However, a widely acknowledged role for marketing during this period is to provide a monitoring function of the market situation. Basically the need for this arises from the common-sense point that, during a perhaps lengthy period of development, the original circumstances favouring the project may change. Such change could be of various types, for example socio-economic or fashion changes, or the unpredicted intrusion of a competitor into the field. Some developments (for example Concorde) take so long that fundamental change in the market-place is wholly unavoidable.

However, if one pursues the Concorde example, it is clear that a great many factors, particularly political ones, will influence decisions about proceeding or not. Termination of a project may be thought obligatory on marketing grounds, but be regarded as unthinkable on political ones, for example because too much taxpayers' money has been spent (but obviously such a point ignores the economist's concept of 'sunk' costs – it is only future costs and revenues which should be considered), or because prestige would be lost (for example with the French), or because, having spent so much, spending 'a little more' might make the difference.

In the case of projects in private industry, pressures will sometimes exist to pursue development when commercial sense might dictate otherwise. The frequently mentioned 'product champion' – an individual, perhaps a high-ranking one in a firm, who has strong faith in an idea (his brain-child), and is anxious to 'push' it – may be able to see a technical development through to fruition despite opposition from marketing and perhaps hostility from the accountancy function. There may be no guarantee of reaching an automatic checkpoint at which a development is terminated. Also let it be added, and this is part of the perpetual frustration but perhaps also the fascination of studying innovative behaviour in firms, the product champion may succeed elaborately, perhaps because having 'held out' so long, the market situation sways in his favour.

In short we do not want to convey any impression of quasi-mechanical go/no-go decisions necessarily being taken on the receipt of adverse market intelligence during development. On the other hand, it is important that firms should monitor their market environments, and some will undoubtedly, and correctly, slow down, modify, or halt a programme if the economic/competitive situation seems to warrant it. But it is important to bear in mind the pressures to persist with development, not least the desire by engineering personnel to solve complex technical problems for their own sake.

It is also as well to dwell on some of the unpredictable aspects of technical development, apart from the difficulty of foretelling exactly when a particular technical problem will be solved. What is not often emphasised is that user requirements may not lend themselves easily to assessment and may actually change during development. In other words, in some cases demand will be a function of the stage of technical development reached. In so far as technical development itself, that is the solution of numerous technical problems on the road to perfecting a prototype, cannot be predicted, then important dimensions of market demand remain equally unpredictable. This argument bears a similarity to a point made earlier, namely that a difficult problem of market assessment of a new product is that demand may be a function of the product – one cannot, in such a case, fully gauge demand until the product is commercialised. (It is not, of course, suggested that such a situation will arise in all instances.) In the case of technical development, the progressive advancement towards a final technical solution may be accompanied by a progressive advancement in users' expectations of the product, leading them to make repeated changes in their evaluation of it. It may be useful to illustrate this and related problems of market assessment by using a case study.

A Case Example

The case relates to the development of a flying field scanner system for automatic detection of surface blemishes in metal sheet and strip.[13] The design objective was the attainment of automatic detection of all those defects which influence the classification of the finished sheet or strip. In this way it was hoped to provide an automatic system of classification to replace the present labour-intensive inspection process in sheet mills.

The development commenced in close co-operation with aluminium-sheet-producing plants. Development work led in time to the stage of a well-engineered system suitable for extended works trials and with the power to detect most of the defects considered significant. An important element of the project was the conduct of intermediate works trials of the system.

These trials involved considerable preparation in order to get an adequate number of typical sheets available at the plant for running through the inspection equipment. This work highlighted the special problems of developing an apparatus for objective quality appraisal to replace a subjective one.

The basic difficulty was that the criteria used in subjective assessment could not be described adequately by the human inspector to enable a satisfactory specification to be written for the automatic inspection device. The result was that as the performance of the apparatus progressed, the user's specification continually extended to expect more or different defects to be recognised – a type of development and testing exercise which could be called a 'creeping specification'.

The apparatus developed and tested was considered by the aluminium-strip producer to meet most of his needs for automatic detection. However, this performance was only obtainable on *oil-free* sheets. Sheets in such condition were not provided at the required inspection station, in accordance with existing mill practice. The developer had, however, anticipated that they would be available by this point in time.

The adoption of the instrument in such an aluminium-sheet-producing plant was thus seen as being dependent upon future development of sheet mill practice. It was felt that this development would probably be associated with this particular inspection problem, activities in the future having to be directed, first to finding aluminium sheet or other non-ferrous sheet production situations to which the current level of the technology would be applicable and, second to raising the speed of inspection capability to five or ten times the present level. (Numerous other product inspection problems were in fact attempted using the same basic technology.)

The above illustrates the importance of accurate prediction of changes in industry process technology, in so far as this is possible. Similar problems present themselves on the market side. The example will be pursued to illustrate the point.

A widening of the potential area of use of the inspection system was undertaken in the hope of an ultimate reasonable return on the relatively high R and D costs involved in pursuing the innovation.

Early in the aluminium-inspection activity the requirement for automatic inspection for glazed ceramic tiles was identified, and this led to the development of a system which was then installed for testing in a tile factory. After some months of trial in routine use the system was considered 'promising but insufficiently consistent in behaviour'. It was felt, however, that further development of the system could be undertaken, but before extra work could be started, the economic situation of the U.K. tile industry had deteriorated, and plants were running seriously under capacity. Further refinements of the system were thus discontinued.

Investigation of the inspection requirements of the tile-making industries in Italy and West Germany, who are major producers, suggested a 'fairly strong' demand for automatic inspection, but mainly for pattern-glazed tiles rather than the plain-coloured tiles to which the system was applicable. The system thus showed little promise of success because of a change of fashion which the product had to adapt itself to meet, apart altogether from the deterioration of the U.K. tile market.

Let us comment briefly on some of the implications of this case. In this instance development and market-testing work went hand in hand. However, the example of the ceramics industry indicated a poor appreciation of the developing situation in a prospective user's end market. and a failure to generate market intelligence during the actual prototype trials themselves. Obviously market study could have been undertaken at an even earlier point and perhaps have led to a decision not to develop a system for this industry, assuming the desired information could have been obtained by market study.

The case also indicates the consequences of conducting market-assessment work after development and testing decisions have been taken rather than before. The decision to investigate the Italian and West German markets at such a late stage and then only to discover an absence of suitable applications is scarcely an ideal way to proceed. It is true that market-research work might equally be wasteful if conducted prematurely, for example before it is known whether trials will be successful. On the other hand, some modest desk research during the aluminium plant trials might have given an earlier warning of the way the tile market was going in European countries.

The situation met with in the aluminium industry also underlines the importance of knowledge of changes in industry process technology to which a proposed new product or system is to be applied. In an atmosphere of uncertainty (and taking full advantage of hindsight) it would appear that this innovator was over-optimistic as to the future development of aluminium sheet mill practice. Perhaps a more pessimistic view would have led to the development of an even lower-technology product with possibly wider application. There is much to recommend a product-development policy which rejects dramatic newness.

The planning of the marketing and sales activities of the commercialisation stage of new-product development is properly the concern of the next chapter. However, an aspect of this activity is introduced here because of its close connection with the 'creeping specification' problem mentioned above.

Where a specification has a tendency to advance, there is a case for arresting the process by identifying a state of development of the new product for a product of that specification in as wide a market as is appropriate to it.

Such an exercise would, of course, depend upon reaching a successful point in development, that is a point at which ability to meet the needs of a user, or group of users, could be demonstrated. Further development to meet this 'creeping specification' could be continued subsequently as a separate exercise.

THE IMPORTANCE OF TECHNICAL DEVELOPMENT/MARKETING CO-ORDINATION

Just as design needs to be co-ordinated adequately with the company's marketing function, so too does technical development require such liaison. This is clearly a major lesson from the above case study.

Support for the need for close ties is provided by different writers, of whom Malmlow is but one example.[14] Although writing from a corporate-planning stance, Malmlow states that the most common observation about technical development made by chief executives when first contemplating strategic planning is that development personnel have very little contact and no co-ordination with the marketing function. In part because of the increasing expensiveness of the successive stages of development, Malmlow states that one 'cannot allow' the technical R and D effort to proceed 'before the marketing function has had a chance to evaluate the potential for a new product, process, or service'. Equally important, the financial and other administrative functions must evaluate the project from their viewpoint before any new phase is decided upon.

Thus Malmlow suggests that firms should ideally carry out each development phase in such a way that interested participants from each major business function are involved to the degree necessary for a balanced and comprehensive effort in each phase. He suggests that one person be appointed as responsible project leader for the phase to be entered, and colleagues from other functions should support him to the extent programmed in advance and approved by all supervisors concerned.

In this way Malmlow sees the entire work programme for the technical R and D function becoming an integral part of the corporate plan, with no discord between any parts of the efforts and the aims of top management.

Attractive though this appears in theory, in practice while such an approach may afford internal satisfaction that effective functional liaison is being achieved, there remain perhaps intractable problems of market assessment, already discussed in the chapter, calling for the exercise of informed judgement by management.

CONCLUSION

A major theme of this chapter has been the importance of effective liaison between design and technical development and the marketing function. It is hoped that a reasonable case has been argued for believing that the end-result of marketable designs can be achieved in a variety of ways using a variety of informational inputs. There does seem to be a need to combine the creativity of the individual designer with the impartial fact gathering of the market-research function.

Equally, technical-development activity must be supported by on-going monitoring of the changing market environment. That such an activity may be fraught with uncertainty (see the example of the field scanner system above) does not invalidate it – it merely emphasises its importance.

Chapter 9

Commercialisation and Beyond

INTRODUCTION

In the previous chapter we took the embryonic product two vital steps nearer the market-place by discussing the problems of designing it and developing it technically. In particular, we emphasised the role of marketing at these two important stages.

With the product available in prototype form, managements would now like answers to certain basic questions before committing themselves to final market launch. In particular, they would prefer to have some advance idea of likely consumer reaction to the product as such, as well as some prior indication of 'real-life' conditions likely to be encountered in the market itself. Such requirements are met by indulging in different forms of product and market testing.

This chapter examines these pre-launch problems, and deals briefly with problems of the launch itself. In addition, attention is also directed to the question of retiral of obsolete products.

Let us therefore commence this chapter by focusing on product and market-testing aspects of new-product development. Specifically we mean to deal with three specific areas under the headings:

(1) concept testing;
(2) product testing; and
(3) test marketing.

Before looking at these in detail, we can record briefly that concept testing is concerned with gauging customer reaction to the idea or concept of a product, the product not necessarily being fully developed. Product testing refers to the situation where some specimens or prototypes of the product exist and are to be exposed to the experience of respondents. Test marketing is the carrying out of a general trial of the proposed marketing-mix associated with the new product in a regionally limited area.

CONCEPT TESTING

The nature of this type of testing can be illustrated by using an example. This is derived from the experience of Findus (West Germany) and is described by Peter Iff.[1] He discusses his experience in connection with the product 'Schlemmerfilet', a frozen fish block topped with breadcrumbs and spices.

This product was examined and refused by all important Findus companies (with the exception of West Germany) mainly because of two factors established by market research. First, housewives are used to eating fish mainly with potatoes and green salad and not with the ingredients contained in 'Schlemmerfilet'. Second, housewives would most likely not be prepared to pre-heat the oven for half an hour and then bake the product in not less than forty minutes; in general, frozen foods only have a good chance of success when preparation time is short (only a few minutes). In this connection, Iff notes that many frozen products intended for cold consumption had to be withdrawn from the market in the past because the long thawing time was unacceptable.

In short, these two factors individually considered seemed to be reason enough to reject the project as far as Findus (West Germany) were concerned. However, Iff reports that when the whole product concept was submitted to housewives, it was accepted by 'the great majority'. The disadvantages and psychological inhibitions were seen as being less important than the advantages the product offered, namely outstandingly good and new taste, new way of eating fish, a prepared food product which was even accepted by people who do not normally eat fish and so on.

This example shows, in Iff's view, how dangerous it can be to abandon an idea before the concept-test stage. As he states, only a first test, in which the idea is presented as part of a whole concept, 'can tell whether it is likely to be a future success or whether there is no hope in continuing the development work'.[2] In the event Findus continued the development work on Schlemmerfilet and when it was introduced in the autumn of 1968 sales were ten times greater than anticipated.

The foregoing case raises a number of issues in connection with concept testing which we should consider. In particular, one is prompted to ask the following:

(1) What is meant by the term 'concept'?

(2) When should a new-product idea undergo a concept test?

(3) What are the objectives of concept testing?

(4) What methods are appropriate?

(5) How should one interpret the results of this testing?

(6) What are the major advantages and limitations of concept testing?

Let us deal briefly with each of these questions below.

(1)   *The meaning of the term 'concept'*

Generally this will vary from case to case, but Iff's view is that whatever is submitted to a concept test should certainly be beyond the stage of a vague idea or simply a new recipe. The test is better the nearer it is to the final product, covering all elements of the marketing-mix.

In practice, this means that the new-product concept should include as far as possible the finished product itself (recipe, handmade samples), the size and shape of portions and of packaging, the price category (definite idea of consumer price), the name, the target group, a unique selling proposition, and – will the idea fit into an existing product range, or is it something completely new?

In addition, Iff points out that some companies will add the following conditions: Does the envisaged consumer price compare reasonably with perhaps rough calculations by the company as to development, manufacturing, marketing and other costs? Can the product be produced in large quantities without undue problems of manufacture?

(2) *When should an idea be concept-tested?*

Generally, Findus, if we take this company as an example, follow the rule that if a new product represents simply an addition to an existing range (the concept of which was obviously accepted by the consumer), the concept stage is left out; only 'real' innovations are concept-tested.

However, this simple rule has not been found completely reliable. Thus in cases where the new product (for example addition of smaller peas to an existing pea range) is presented to the market with various elements of its marketing-mix altered (for example different packaging, different price, and so on), it has to be decided whether the whole product concept is now changed. If so, a concept test may be obligatory.

(3) *The objectives of concept testing*

Iff[3] provides a detailed listing of the questions to which concept testing should provide answers, and it will be helpful to summarise the main ones here:

Basis acceptance of the idea, respectively of the new product and its concept (as many marketing elements determined as possible);

If basically not or not well accepted, why not?

Does the new idea fit into existing consumption habits or does it follow at least the trend in which consumption habits seem to be changing? (But Iff warns that this point 'might all of a sudden become irrelevant' if new consumption habits are provoked by the appearance of a new product.)

Does the product fill a gap in the offering of similar products?

Judgement on the various product characteristics;

Possible advantages for consumers; do these advantages correspond to the advantages foreseen for the product before the test? Or are there advantages not thought of before?

Buying motivations;

Possible occasions of use – size of portions satisfactory?

Judgement on suggested name – new name proposals;

Idea about suggested price – buying intention on basis of this price;

Are similar products prepared at home? Or is the product spontaneously compared with other similar industrially prepared products?

If yes, how does our product compare with these similar products?

(4) Concept-testing methods

It is beyond the scope of this book to go into method in detail, but one may note briefly the method employed by Findus.[4] Usually about sixty people from the appropriate target group are selected for what is described as 'psychological interviews'. Each interviewee receives the test product at home for a few days before the interview, prepares it, and uses it with the family. The product is tasted again during the interview which lasts, on average, one hour per person.[5]

In the industrial market well-established techniques such as personal interviews, telephone interviews and questionnaire surveys, as well as trial usage are employed in testing new-product concepts. The choice of methods, the relative contribution of each, and the sequence in which they are carried out varies according to the market situation involved. Thus an initial mail questionnaire may be used to pre-test questions that will ultimately be asked in personal interviews. Again, a company may first contact key customers by personal interview then contact others by mail later.[6]

(5) Judging the results of concept testing

Iff[7] states that one has to decide whether test results are positive (justifying continuation of the project) or negative (calling for termination of the project).

Generally, positive results have been attained when, the product idea has, in principle, been 'well accpted' by the majority of respondents, and when the product 'really shows some exciting aspects' which other, similar, products do not have, and could therefore form 'an interesting product story'. If both these points are not fulfilled, Iff's view is that the test results should be regarded as negative.

Given positive results, the new-product idea is further

developed and prepared for the next step, namely the product test, to which we now turn. However, before leaving concept testing, let us briefly highlight its major advantages and disadvantages.

(6) *Advantages and limitations of concept testing*

The major advantages of this type of testing are perhaps fairly self-evident, and largely flow from the assistance given to managements to form early judgements on the likelihood of market success of new ideas. On the other hand, certain limitations exist, including the risk of disclosure of company plans to competitors.

For convenience we reproduce a summary of advantages and limitations which are set out in Table 9.1. Although relating to industrial goods, many of these points are germane to consumer goods also.

TABLE 9.1 *Advantages and limitations of product-concept testing*

REPORTED ADVANTAGES

It enables planners to form early judgement as to the likelihood of market success for a proposed product, before the company has committed itself to a definite course of action and, perhaps, considerable investment.

It can be used to evaluate the relative merits of several new-product proposals, and to decide on the most advantageous allocation of developmental and marketing resources.

It gives management a checkpoint at which it can determine whether the best course is to abandon, revise, or proceed with the proposed project.

It can uncover preliminary clues as to: desirability of specific product attributes; probable markets, applications and users of the product; reactions of prospects to the product idea; pricing possibilities; marketing, sales, promotional, and physical distribution considerations; and, possibly, rough indications of the market's size.

It provides the company with a product 'blueprint' which can be used as a guide by marketing and development units in making their plans and preparing for the next stage of testing or review.

REPORTED LIMITATIONS

It entails some risk of disclosing company plans to competitors.

Time and expense are required for the planning and carrying out of concept testing.

Respondents may find it difficult to grasp the idea for a non-existent product, and to visualise its application as well as their own future needs for it.

Some respondents, having nothing at stake, may overstate their actual interest and thereby encourage unsound development.

Some respondents may resist full co-operation at this stage, fearing that this would somehow imply a commitment to purchase the product once it was developed.

The validity of any measure of potential market size obtained through early-stage concept testing is often dubious.

Any or all of the findings could be misleading if the test is not carried out properly.

For many reasons, some just noted, the test results are necessarily tentative and inconclusive.

Source: M. B. MacDonald, Jr, *Appraising the Market for New Industrial Products*, Business Policy Study, No. 123, National Industrial Conference Board (New York) p. 40.

PRODUCT TESTING

Penny, Hunt and Twyman[8] suggest that, following some experience of a product, respondents in a product-testing situation can be asked various questions relating to:

(*a*) over-all disposition to the product in terms of evaluation or intention ratings;

(*b*) perception of product attributes in terms of ratings or reasons for (*a*);

(*c*) comparative discrimination or preference judgement against a product previously experienced or currently experienced in 'real life'; and

(*d*) comparative discrimination or preference judgement against a product previously or currently experienced as part of the test.

Thus the test can vary between reporting characteristics of

an experience either absolutely or comparatively with another experience whose distance in time is another test variable. The experience to be reported upon, these authors state, can vary considerably and can include:

(a) simple sensations like taste or smell;

(b) a complex of sensations as when a whole dish is under test;

(c) a complex of sensations observed in oneself and others, as with a food product tested on a family;

(d) the observed nature of some process carried out by the observer, such as handwashing;

(e) a mixture of observing the nature of a process and reporting on sensations, as with food requiring preparation; and

(f) the observed nature of a process going on in a machine, such as the running of a car.

Where the objective is restricted to finding out the strengths and weaknesses of a product, Dr Jorg Rehorn,[9] on the basis of his testing experience, found that postal tests were completely adequate. While the use of postal methods has limitations in relation to the duration and depth of the interview, Rehorn believes the acceptability of mail questionnaires is in part substantiated by the fact that the two largest institutional product-test panels in West Germany both carry out their tests by post. Rehorn's tests were in all cases *blind tests*, that is the consumer did not know the makers of the products, and the packaging was plain.

On the basis of his experience, Rehorn believes the main types of information sought by product testing can be summarised as follows:

(1) whether there is a preference for the test products;

(2) the over-all impression left by the test products;

(3) the way the test products are rated in comparison with the product normally used;

(4) the readiness to purchase the test products; and

(5) ideas as to prices (readiness to pay the price).

In the absence of guidance from published empirical research, Rehorn has developed five 'decision aids' to be used in conjunction with the five 'assessment criteria' outlined above. These are:

(1) in a comparative test of two products, the test product should achieve a higher preference than the comparison product, the market leader;

(2) at least 40 per cent of those participating should give the over-all rating 'very good';

(3) at least one-third of those taking part in the test should consider the test product as better than the one they were previously using;

(4) more than one-half should express the opinion that they would 'definitely' like to buy the test product; and

(5) the average amount they are prepared to pay should not be lower than the actual price to final consumers.

The more of these requirements the test result satisfies and the better it satisfies them, the greater is the probability that the test product, if marketed, will not fail *because of its qualities as a product.*

TEST MARKETING

The result of a product test should never be viewed in isolation. It is simply one device among those which can be used to reduce the risk of a market launch. Even where it shows the product to possess a high quality, market failure is still a possibility if other important factors in the marketing-mix show weakness. It is therefore logical for us to examine how the company's total marketing-mix may be tested, using test-marketing methods.

As Rodger[11] suggests, experience indicates that the chances of a new product being successful are 'significantly greater' if it is first put into a controlled test market where it is exposed to realistic competitive conditions. In support of this view he points to the evidence collected over many years by the A. C. Nielsen marketing-research organisation who have consistently advocated adequate test marketing of new ideas.

While the test market should provide some indication of probable success or failure, it should also seek to identify the specific factors most likely to contribute to the success of the product, as well as the most appropriate combination of marketing-mix elements. As Rodger emphasises, there is no mystique about test marketing – what matters is the effective planning and management of the test market, and the analysis and interpretation of the results.

Let us go into these and related matters in more detail, and consider the following:

(1) the objectives of test marketing;
(2) guidelines for effective test marketing;
(3) pitfalls of test marketing;
(4) the validity of test marketing; and
(5) The contribution of test marketing to new product success.

(1) *The objectives of test marketing*

Davis[12] suggests that the objectives of test marketing fall into two major categories, which he calls the 'mechanical' and the 'commercial'.

The mechanical aspect, which in his view is frequently overlooked by manufacturers, is concerned with the opportunities afforded the tester to assess such matters as his own arrangements for handling and storing materials, producing and despatching the product in good condition, and assessing suppliers.

The commercial aspect operates from the factory onwards, and is concerned with the way traders and consumers receive the new product. Broadly the objective is to assess if the marketing-mix under test will

(*a*) give adequate distribution in shops,
(*b*) give a sufficient flow of people trying the product, and
(*c*) give sufficient sales through repeat purchase to indicate the likelihood of national success.

Basically the test market is carried out by scaling down the operation to a small area, typically a television area, in which a 'mini' marketing operation is carried out.

(2)   *Guidelines for effective test marketing*

The A. C. Nielsen organisation mentioned above has distilled many years of test-marketing experience into a series of 'lessons' designed to assist the would-be tester to obtain maximum value from his researchers. These are reproduced below: [13]

(*a*)   design the test to find an answer to a single major issue;
(*b*)   incorporate the test into an over-all marketing plan;
(*c*)   set targets at same level as national expectations;
(*d*)   be completely objective in evaluating results;
(*e*)   benefit from comparative testing where possible;
(*f*)   profit from professional advice;
(*g*)   select a representative area;
(*h*)   allow sufficient time to set up the test properly;
(*i*)   establish a test base against which to measure subsequent changes;
(*j*)   carefully analyse competitors' market shares;
(*k*)   welcome exposure to competitive retaliation during the test;
(*l*)   examine retailer co-operation and support;
(*m*)   examine repeat sales pattern;
(*n*)   co-ordinate advertising and promotion;
(*o*)   avoid using methods during the test which will not be repeated during the expansion period;
(*p*)   evaluate all possible factors which influence sales;
(*q*)   avoid interference with the test once it is launched;
(*r*)   adjust results to changes which may occur in the market prior to expansion or market launch;
(*s*)   allow sufficient time for the test to mature and for the results to be analysed; and
(*t*)   employ proper research procedures, and budget to allow sample size and design indicated by the test problem.

While it is Nielsen's experience that products which meet targets set in test markets 'seldom fail to repeat this pattern, when launched nationally', they emphasise that this result 'does not come about by chance', there being many pitfalls which have to be avoided.[14] It is to some of these that we now turn.

(3) *Some common pitfalls of test marketing*

Rodger[15] summarises some of the more frequent planning and organisational failures made in test marketing, and it may be useful to outline his points here. Before doing so, however, it should be noted that 'bad' test-marketing practice will be the obverse of the points made in the above section. Bearing this in mind, Rodger's points are as follows:

(*a*) Failure to decide what is to be tested. Each test should try to answer a major question, for example the most effective weight for advertising. Where one attempts to test several factors in a single test area, the more difficult it is to identify the *real* causes of success or failure.

(*b*) Failure to base the test-market plan on an over-all national marketing plan which is both realistic and affordable.

(*c*) Failure to make comparative tests.

(*d*) Failure to establish bench-marks in the test area. Before any test begins it is necessary to establish individual and total sales and/or market penetration of competitive brands so that subsequent changes can then be compared and evaluated against this base.

(*e*) Failure to select representative test areas.

(*f*) Failure to adhere to the test-market plan.

(*g*) Failure to consider and get objective and reliable data on all factors influencing sales results in the test area.

(*h*) Failure to stay in the test market long enough to get a clear-cut stop or go decision.

(*i*) Reading into test-market results more than is supportable by the objective facts.

(4) *The validity of test marketing*

Given the manifold difficulties facing the company indulging in test marketing, it is not surprising that managements should be concerned with the validity of results obtained.

Davis[16] addresses the question of the purely statistical validity of test marketing, and finds that test marketing tends to be statistically invalid from the outset. On what grounds does he base this assertion?

Davis argues that where, as frequently happens, test marketing is restricted to one area, a basic principle of sound experimental design is violated, namely the need for replication. Replication, in the case of test marketing (meaning the conduct of tests in two areas and not simply one), enables the consequences of an atypical area to be avoided, and comparisons to be made. However, according to Davis, such benefits are frequently forgone, in part because of the attractions of using television areas as test areas. Thus one is unlikely to replicate a test where as much as perhaps one-tenth of the entire country is involved.

Thus Davis believes that test marketing's foundation in statistical theory is not particularly sound, and he urges test statisticians to strive for better research designs. However, his general view is that such testing has obvious value – one cannot discard it merely because it is difficult to apply.

(5) *The contribution of test marketing to new-product success*

Although a large and growing battery of techniques, including mock-up supermarkets and controlled tests in individual towns, are available to firms contemplating test marketing, it is as well to bear in mind the high failure rate of new products as emphasised in Chapter 1. Superficially it would appear that test marketing cannot guarantee new-product success.

It is perhaps not surprising, therefore, that many companies are not now troubling with exhaustive test marketing, preferring to rely on product and packaging tests and then committing full resources to 'roll-out' regional launches. This is the view taken by the Marketing Editor of the *Financial Times* who stated: 'The feeling is that if you are going to invest in the production equipment, and the expense of a regional TV advertising campaign, there is little point in pussyfooting.'[17]

The reader will not fail to notice the contrast between this statement and the views of the A. C. Nielsen organisation (see above) who stress the essentiality of test marketing. Who is right?

Some light may be thrown on this by quoting some recent research by Nielsen and referred to in the *Financial Times* article. In 1968 Nielsen followed 46 brands in test and found that only 44 per cent of them proved good enough to go national. In 1973 there had been little improvement. Of 34 brands researched on test market only 47 per cent made further progress. In other words, half the new products failed *in test*.

Superficially this does not appear to support the cause of test marketing. What is required is an indication of brand performance after launch. Nielsen provides this also.

They assumed that new brands would be judged as successes if they achieved nationally at least 80 per cent of the market share they gained on test. In 1968, 87 per cent of the brands which were sold nationally matched their test performance; in 1973 all did. One may therefore conclude that where test marketing is used, a product stands on average a 90 per cent chance of succeeding nationally.

Despite such impressive statistics, some firms still eschew the test-marketing stage, sometimes with very good reason. Thus Cadbury Schweppes decided to enter the soup market with a range of 'make in the cup soups' (called Cadbury's snack soups) without a preliminary test market.[18] This was partly motivated by the likelihood of other soup companies launching similar lines, in some cases fully test marketed. Thus, although some companies will be conscious of the advantages of test marketing, the need to take rapid market action may be one factor preventing them from doing so.

LAUNCHING NEW PRODUCTS

In Chapter 1 we introduced the concept of a product life cycle and argued that a new product passes through a series of phases analogous to the stages through which living organisms pass between birth and death. In the case of the product we characterised the main phases as introduction, growth, maturity and decline. We also noted that, while the product life-cycle concept is of great value in that it reflects the nature of the process through which the sales of a new product pass, its main deficiency lies in the fact that it tells us nothing about the time frame involved.

Despite this latter deficiency it has been argued at length[19] that the consistent shape of the product life cycle, or in a wider context the diffusion curve, suggests that there is some basic underlying process which, if properly understood, might be put to good use by the marketer.

In essence the regularity of the diffusion curve is believed to arise from the fact that adoption/diffusion depends upon contact between an adopter and another adopter, and that such contact will assume the form of a geometric progression. One does not require an advanced knowledge of the theory of probability to appreciate that if adoption is dependent upon contact between adopter and non-adopter then each contact will double the probability of further contact until 50 per cent of the population have become adopters, whereafter the probability that any given contact will be with a non-adopter will diminish in a symmetrical manner.

If one wished to predict the speed with which a new product would diffuse, the critical piece of information is the length of time it will take the seller to establish contact with the first adopter. In most physical processes it is usually possible to predict this time lag with considerable accuracy due to known regularities in the behaviour of members of the population in which the reaction is introduced. Unfortunately, human behaviour is less predictable, and in most marketing situations there is considerable uncertainty *a priori* as to the ultimate size of the adopter population. In many cases one can make a reasonably accurate estimate of the proportion of the total population who are likely to be users of a new product and this is usually considered to be the potential demand for it. However, in order to translate potential demand into effective demand, it is necessary to do more than merely make contact with potential users and communicate one's selling proposition to them. In fact, once one has pre-identified a population of potential adopters it is tautologous to point out that only one of them can be the first adopter. A very large number of studies in the field of rural and medical sociology, and more lately in consumer marketing, have shown that the first adopters or innovators are often markedly different from later adopters although there is insufficient regularity in these differentiating factors to enable the identification of an innovator 'type', that is early adoption is to some extent dependent upon the exact context of the adoption decision.

F

The foregoing discussion suggests certain normative decision rules for management. The first is that although an estimate of potential demand may be sufficient to justify the development of a new product, it is insufficient to ensure that the firm's marketing efforts are directed to the most receptive members of this potential market who are most likely to be amongst the first to try and adopt the new product when it is introduced into the market-place. If, therefore, we are to ensure rapid acceptance and diffusion it is clear that we must try and pre-determine what factors differentiate early adopters for our product category from those who are much slower to make an adoption decision. It is our belief that early adoption is dependent upon both economic and behavioural factors and the relative importance of these will vary according to the magnitude of the economic risk associated with purchase.

The benefit of pre-identifying the potential early adopter is self-evident. It ensures that we can make a direct approach to them rather than waste time in making a random approach to the whole potential market, and it also ensures that we can target our communication strategy directly to their needs. By so doing we enhance the likelihood of establishing early awareness as the first stage in an adoption process, moving through interest, evaluation and trial prior to a final decision to adopt the new product. It is also clear that in the case of product purchases much of the bandwagon or contagion effect results from the reduction in perceived risk on the part of potential buyers when the seller can give evidence concerning the existence of satisfied customers for the same product.

In the space available it is not possible to deal at length with how to set about pre-identifying likely early adopters. For a full discussion on this readers are referred to *Marketing New Industrial Products*.[20]

PRODUCT RETIRAL

The necessity for withdrawing products from the market-place has been implicit throughout our consideration of product management; accordingly, as a postscript to a discussion of marketing new products, it is appropriate that we make some reference to the product-retiral decision.

As suggested, the need to eliminate products from the product line has been implicit in both our acceptance of the product life-cycle concept and in our emphasis upon the need to develop new products, not only as a means to growth but also as replacements for those which have ceased to earn satisfactory profits. However, while the decision to retire old products is equally as important as the decision to introduce new ones, it has received comparatively little attention in the marketing literature. In part this is probably attributable to the absence of novelty and excitement associated with a new-product launch, heightened by the uncertainty as to whether or not the product will succeed at all. By contrast, retirement and death are ultimately inevitable and the objective seems to be to achieve this with the minimum of unseemly fuss. As a result it seems to us that such decisions may often be made without full consideration of all the factors involved, particularly when it is appreciated that products which have passed maturity and begun to decline have by definition enjoyed a successful life – if they had not, the issue would not arise. It follows that the firm already has extensive and valuable knowledge of marketing such products and it is argued that full use should be made of this information.

These comments should not be construed as implying that management is in danger of eliminating large numbers of products prematurely. On the contrary the reverse is often true. Established products have many 'friends', both within the producing company and among its customers, and vested interest may well prolong life long after the product has ceased to make a positive contribution to the firm's over-all profitability. Essentially, therefore, we take the view that product retiral should be based on as formal an analysis as that used to select new products for development. Similarly, we believe that the firm should assign specific responsibility for reviewing product performance to a person or committee not directly involved with marketing the product itself, and should develop both objective criteria and formal guidelines concerning the weight to be attached to non-quantifiable aspects of a product's performance, for example having a 'full' line of products, complementarily with other products, and so forth.

Ideally the review of a product's performance should be conducted on a regular basis and may usefully be broken down into two phases. The first of these phases should be a relatively simple screening test to establish whether or not a product is in good health, while the second would consist of a more exhaustive investigation of those items failing to pass the screening test.

In one of the most thoughtful discussions of product retiral, Alexander,[21] suggests six criteria for use in screening the product line – *sales, prices,* and *profit* trends, *substitute products, product effectiveness,* and *executive time.*

A downward trend in sales, price and/or profits may all indicate that a product is in trouble – the important thing is to determine whether such trends reflect a fundamental change in the environment or are merely due to temporary fluctuations. Further, a downturn in any or all of these objective indicators will usually be found to be associated with one or other of Alexander's remaining three criteria. For example, if costs are properly imputed to executive time then the need to allocate more of this resource to nursing a sick product will be apparent in the profit calculation. On the other hand, while substitute products will inevitably erode an original product's *share* of total demand, it is quite conceivable that, in an expanding and buoyant market, price and sales may remain stable and belie the existence of such competition. Accordingly, we suggest that *market share* be added to the list of diagnostic indicators.

Although sales, price, market share and profit are all interrelated, it is useful to try and obtain values for each of these parameters for, as suggested by our market-share example, it is quite possible to have *contra* indications which would not be apparent if only one measure were available (for example a declining market may result from a deliberate policy to raise price and 'skim' a market, in which case one would expect sales to decline while profits increase). Similarly, one should seek to establish a basis for comparison with some other readily available indicator, such as the over-all level of profits in the firm or industry, the rate of growth in the economy as a whole, and so on.

Assuming that the indicators suggest a decline in a product's contribution, then the next step must be a full evaluation of its performance. Generalisations as to how one should approach such an analysis are apt to be dangerous for the simple reason that every product, firm and market is in some sense unique. While this does not prevent the identification of useful guidelines their application should be tempered by reference to the specific context of each particular decision.

In the case of a single-product firm it is clear that sales, costs, profits and so on, are all direct measures of that product's performance – it is also evident that it would usually be unacceptable to propose that a single-product firm should immediately drop its product given a decline in sales and/or profits. To do so would be equivalent to liquidation. On the other hand, a similar recommendation to a multi-product company might be perfectly acceptable. However, where a firm is producing a wide range of products it is often difficult to be certain just what is the contribution of any individual item, and marginal analysis can only help if one can define the margin (usually one cannot!). Problems of joint costs and overhead allocation are more the province of a text on cost accountancy,[22] but it must be recognised that to some degree all such allocations are based upon value judgements. Accordingly, one should carefully reassess the nature and effect of the original value judgement which gave rise to the existing scheme of cost allocation to determine whether or not they hold good under the new situation (an apparent decline in one product's performance). Similarly, one must consider how the costs borne by a deleted product will be reallocated, and what impact such reallocation might have, prior to dropping the doubtful item, for example in reducing the gross margin on the remaining products. Thus, as Alexander points out[23] one must be careful not to adopt too simplified an approach, such as dropping all products whose profits are below average – by definition the average is the central measure of dispersion so some dispersion must exist. Accordingly, if the average profit is acceptable, it might be better to accept this gratefully rather than drop below-average performers only to find that in some way the above-average performers owed this distinction to a joint relationship which is thereby destroyed.

Added to and allied with problems of joint cost allocation in multi-product firms is the question of the fixed cost directly associated with manufacture of a particular product (clearly in a single-product firm all fixed costs may be ascribed to the product). Where the fixed assets may be redeployed, liquidated, or are fully depreciated, the problem is easily resolved but, where the fixed assets are product specific and do not fall into one of the three categories mentioned, product-retiral decisions are complicated. Essentially, there is a trade off between contribution to fixed costs or overhead, which might defer retirement, and the concept of sunk cost which might predicate immediate withdrawal so that managerial time and effort could be better concentrated on the remaining or replacement products.

Under more enlightened personnel policies, and especially where the labour force is highly skilled, there is a growing tendency to regard employees as a fixed cost, at least in the medium term. It follows, therefore, that in assessing the impact of product retiral upon the company's capital one must also consider the impact upon its labour force. Ideally management will have been following the planned approach to product management recommended in this book and will have a mix of products at various stages in their life cycle so that as one declines another grows to replace it thus maintaining a high level of utilisation of all the company's resources. But where a company has no other product available to absorb the resources freed by a product retiral, then clearly it is better to retain the declining item, so long as it covers its variable costs and makes some contribution to fixed costs. The company can then use this 'breathing space' to develop replacement products.

Thus far our discussion has assumed that a continuing decline in sales, profit and/or market share presage a product-deletion decision – an assumption supported by the shape of the classic product life-cycle curve. However, as has been pointed out elsewhere,[24] an analysis of biological life cycles would suggest that decline is not inevitable when an organism comes against a ceiling to its continued growth. Many organisms achieve a remarkable stability analogous to that enjoyed by long-lived products (Guinness, mild steel?) while others mutate in a manner which enables them to escape the limiting condition and recommence another growth cycle. In product terms, stabilisation is usually dependent upon a policy of continuous modification and improvement to counteract erosion of demand by the development of substitutes, while regeneration may follow from innovation in marketing (finding new user) or in a radical change in the product itself which creates new demand for it (for example Instamatic and Polaroid cameras).

However, assuming that it is not possible to extend the product life cycle through innovation, and the decline in its contribution to the firm's product-mix continues, there may be no alternative to retirement. Once this decision has been made the prime concern must be to achieve the deletion with the minimum inconvenience both to the firm and its customers. The factors to be borne in mind will vary with the type of product but in every case where a long-established product is to be withdrawn the producer should communicate the fact to the channels of distribution and the ultimate consumer with as much advance warning as possible. In the case of convenience goods, notification will probably suffice although it may be necessary to offer discounts to move any remaining stocks. But in the case of durable goods (consumer or industrial) the manufacturer will usually have to make additional arrangements for parts and replacements, and ensure the continued availability of after-sales service to avoid losing customer goodwill.

In conclusion we would reiterate the point stressed so frequently in the preceding pages, and especially in the context of new product development, namely that a structured analysis of the issues and the setting down of a formal plan for action will invariably pay handsome dividends.

Chapter 10

American Motors Corporation – A Case Study in Product Policy

INTRODUCTION

At the Harvard Business School one of the more famous cases in the compulsory second-year Business Policy course is American Motors Corporation[1] – a case which describes the fortunes of the smallest of the four national automobile manufacturers in the United States during the period between 1954 and the end of 1962. Although its inclusion at the beginning of the Business Policy course is predicated on the grounds that it offers an early opportunity for students to gain familiarity with the concept of corporate strategy, its inclusion in this book is justified on the grounds that it provides an excellent insight into the relationship between product policy and the firm's over-all strategy. It also illustrates the practical application of a number of the principles discussed in the earlier chapters in a more abstract fashion.

PRODUCT POLICY IN THE U.S. AUTOMOBILE INDUSTRY

As is the case in most new industries, the early years of the U.S. car industry were characterised by a production orientation in which the main emphasis was upon the technical development of the innovation with little or no attention given to the possibility of differentiating demand on the basis of consumer preferences. Entry to the industry was relatively easy and a large number of producers set up in business each of whom was convinced that their own product was exactly what the market was looking for.

While the varied offerings of these essentially small-scale producers did much to stimulate primary demand for the new product category 'motor-car' their inefficient methods of manufacture resulted in a very high unit cost which effectively put the product beyond the purchasing power of the average consumer. Thus the first decade of the century was characterised by the existence of a very large potential demand for the basic product, if only its price could be brought within the reach of the man in the street. It was the legendary Henry Ford who first recognised the existence of this enormous latent demand and, like the manufacturers spawned by the Industrial Revolution, realised that this potential could be released by producing a standardised output at the lowest possible unit cost. Although we may cite Henry Ford's oft-quoted dictum 'you can have any colour so long as it's black' as the antithesis of everything that marketing stands for, in fact it was a much more accurate reflection of demand at that time than would have been a product policy based upon differentiation. In fact, differentiation was offered by the heterogeneous output of the multitude of other producers in the market, but it was Ford who dominated the market from 1910 right through until 1921 with his Model T to the extent that in the latter year he controlled 62 per cent of total industry sales while the remaining 87 suppliers could only muster 38 per cent between them.

However, 1921 marked the peak of the Ford fortunes for significant changes were beginning to manifest themselves in the market-place. In the immediate aftermath of the First World War the U.S. economy enjoyed a boom in 1919 and 1920. In the latter year Ford had a 45 per cent share of market while its nearest rival, General Motors, was a very poor second with 17 per cent. However, the boom of 1920 was followed by a recession in 1921 with the result that G.M.'s share slumped to 12 per cent while Ford, with its lower-priced Model T, accelerated to 62 per cent. It was as a result of this setback in their fortunes that the Executive Committee of General Motors sat down to formulate a new strategy for the corporation.

The nature and outcome of these deliberations are fully recorded in Alfred P. Sloan Jr's *My Years with General Motors*.[2] However, two quotations will serve to summarise the policy articulated by the Executive Committee which has dominated product policy in the industry to the present day.

In broad terms the Committee was given the corporate objective of competing with Ford in the low-price volume car market. As Sloan comments:

> our answer was to accept the concept of a new car design but to place it in the perspective of a broad product policy. The product policy we proposed is the one for which General Motors has now long been known. We said first that the corporation should produce a line of cars in each price area, from the lowest price up to one for a strictly high-grade quantity production car, but we would not get into the fancy-price field with small production; second, that the price steps should not be such as to leave wide gaps in the line, and yet should be great enough to keep their number within reason, so that the greatest advantage of quantity production could be secured; and third, that there should be no duplication by the corporation in the price fields or steps. These new policies never materialised precisely in this form – for example, we always have had in fact duplication and competition between the divisions – yet essentially the new product policy differentiated the new General Motors from the old, and the new General Motors from the Ford organisation of the time and from other car manufacturers.[3]

A little later in the same chapter Sloan amplifies on the strict interpretation of their product policy in the lowest-price segment where there was the greatest probability of coming into head-on conflict with the then dominant Ford:

> The product policy also took up specifically the problem of penetrating the low-price field, a special case of the general concept. The field for cars of the first grade, we noted, was then practically monopolised by the Ford, and we were trying to invade it. We recommended that General Motors should not attempt to build and sell a car of the precise

Ford level, as the Ford sold at the lowest price within the first grade. Instead the corporation should market a car much better than the Ford, with a view to selling it at or near the top price in the first grade. We did not propose to compete head on with the Ford grade, but to produce a car that would be superior to the Ford, yet so near the Ford price that demand would be drawn from the Ford grade and lifted to the slightly higher price in preference to Ford's then utility design.[4]

The full significance of this quotation will become apparent a little later in our story.

As the United States climbed out of the 1921 slump and entered upon the boom of the mid-1920s it was clear that G.M. had correctly interpreted the signs. Bare transportation – the Model T product concept – was no longer enough to satisfy the increasing affluence of the consumer, and General Motor's policy of offering the highest quality within each price segment paid off dividends to the extent that by 1927 it had captured one-third of the market. At the same time Ford's sales had declined to one-third, a level which was insufficient to enable Ford to operate profitably and so forced him to close down and tool up for his own response to the demand for a better-quality car – the Model A.

Tobe[5] describes subsequent events as follows:

General Motors continued and adopted the basic philosophy that has dominated the automobile industry in the United States, from a product standpoint, until the last few years. As a matter of fact, you'd almost have to say it still dominates in terms of current product volume. But General Motors adopted the policy – clearly stated by their technical people and policy people – of building cars each year a little bigger, a little bit more stylish, for the purpose of progressive, dynamic obsolescence. That product policy, coupled with other contributions they made – because General Motors has made many very substantial and significant contributions to the concepts of large industrial management – made General Motors the largest industrial corporation in the world.

Ford never quite came back. Under Henry Ford Sr, the company never really adopted the product policy of General Motors. But following World War II the new management, in an effort to recapture first place, literally jumped on to the General Motors bandwagon, and basically adopted the General Motors product philosophy.

Then five years ago, when there was a change in the Chrysler management (1953–4), Chrysler did the same thing. By 1954, therefore, at the time of the formation of American Motors, you had the three dominant factors in the automobile industry all going down substantially the identical product road.

As a result of this philosophy of making their cars a little bigger and more powerful each year, they kept moving them up in size and reducing the degree of variation and distinction. The result was that they created a vacuum back of them in the market and they created a concentration of competition as between their own models.

AMERICAN MOTORS AND THE 'COMPACT CAR'

From the point of view of American Motors, formed on 1 May, 1954 from the merger of two declining manufacturers, the Hudson Motor Car Company and Nash–Kelvinator Corporation, this vacuum in the market represented a marketing opportunity of the type discussed in Chapter 4. The manner in which American Motors capitalised on this opportunity is a classic example of the role played by the 'product champion' in introducing an innovation into the market-place, and of the strategy 'attack when the enemy retreats' suggested in Chapter 3.

In this case, the product champion was George Romney, president and chairman of the company since its formation in 1954. (It is not without significance that product champions such as Romney or Alistair Pilkington (Float Glass) already held posts of influence when they espoused their causes and it would be dangerous to assume that anyone with sufficient single-mindedness of purpose could become a successful product champion.) Romney observed the gap at the bottom end

of the market for a car which was intermediate in size between domestically produced cars and the small cars imported
from Europe. Belief in the existence of potential demand for
such a 'compact' car was reinforced in Romney's mind by the
evidence that 85 per cent of all car journeys were less than
thirteen miles in length and undertaken for essential purposes
rather than for pleasure. In fact the car had become an integral part of everyday life to the extent that one might
reasonably infer that the market had come full circle to the
situation identified by Henry Ford half a century before – a
need for low-cost, reliable transportation.

This identification of a market opportunity, and Romney's
declared objective to become a leading competitor in the
automotive field, constituted a clear statement of purpose of
the type recommended in our consideration of strategy in
Chapter 3. At the same time the condition of the company
when it formulated these goals was such that its first task was
to survive. Much of the period between 1954 and 1957 was
in fact occupied with 'campaign survival' during which time
Romney pruned operations to bare essentials while convincing
his own sales organisation and dealers of the acceptability of
the compact-car concept.

While American Motors was struggling for survival, the
Big Three (Ford, General Motors and Chrysler) were heading for a traumatic confrontation of their own making, the
seeds of which had been sown some three years previously.
Essentially the confrontation arose because Ford had tried
trading up into the higher-price ranges which had been dominated by General Motors since the 1920s. Experiencing a
measure of success, Ford committed itself to developing more
models for the medium-price bracket with bigger body shells.
However, a major model change takes between eighteen
months and two years to implement on a current model while
retooling for a completely new model takes three years.
Learning of Ford's plans for a bigger car early in 1955,
General Motors made the decision to opt for one big body
shell for all its models for 1958. (It also hedged its bets by
deciding to introduce a compact of its own in 1959.) However, once Ford and General Motors were committed to
developing still bigger and more powerful cars it began to

become apparent in 1956 that changes were taking place in the market.

Two of the more significant changes which were discerned were resistance to both price and the size of the Buick and Oldsmobile ranges, both of which were manufactured by General Motors and had dominated the medium-priced segments for many years. Traditionally these models had sold best in the big cities and it was a fundamental change in the residential patterns of these cities which precipitated the crisis. In a phrase this change can be summarised as 'the move to suburbia'. One of the consequences of this move was that families found a single car insufficient for their needs but such families could not affort to buy two medium-priced cars. At the same time, congestion in the downtown areas of the cities was exacerbated by the sheer size of the cars themselves and drivers began to look for something more manoeuvrable and easy to park. Thus the general weakness in demand for the G.M. models was exaggerated by Ford's policy of trading up into the bottom end of the price bracket.

Discerning these trends, and noting the success recorded by the imports of small foreign cars, American Motors made an historic decision to drop the famous Nash and Hudson names and concentrate all its efforts behind its compact-car concept sold under the Rambler brand name – a perfect example of the strategy of concentrated marketing discussed in Chapter 3.

Although Romney made it quite clear that 1958 was to be a 'do or die' year for American Motors, he did not allow his belief in the basic concept of the compact car to override his perception of consumer preference. Thus, when asked why the 1958 Rambler had tail fins, a feature he had criticised in other manufacturers' products, he replied: 'It's the basic concept that counts. If we have to use tail fins to get people to try compact cars, we'll use tail fins. Later on we will certainly be able to do away with them, and to build clean, simple, uncluttered cars.'[6] Similarly, Romney had discontinued production of the 100-inch wheelbase Rambler American from 1955 to 1958, on the grounds that initially the 100-inch car represented too great a departure from the traditional U.S. product to be acceptable, while the 108-inch was a smaller departure but sufficient to get across the idea.

The success of American Motors' strategy may be judged by the fact that in October 1958 sales were running at triple the level in the preceding year. In 1959 American Motors achieved a 6 per cent market share and earned pre-tax profits of \$105m., a performance it was to sustain in 1960.

As we noted earlier the Big Three were not insensitive to the changes which stimulated demand for a smaller and cheaper car; their misfortune lay in the fact that they became aware of the trend after they had committed themselves to the production of even bigger models in 1955–6, and the fruit of this decision was not born until 1958. Thus, given their commitment, there was little that the Big Three could do in the immediate short term but sweat it out, capitalise their investment in the big-car lines and put in hand plans for the introduction of their own compacts. The case study,[7] and an article from *Fortune* reported in it, provide a revealing insight into the process of strategy formulation and its implications for product policy.

THE BIG THREE REVISE THEIR STRATEGY

As of 1960 there were signs that the total market for cars had stabilised – in the terms of our product life-cycle concept it had reached maturity. According to this view the market for cars had become largely one for replacement which could be expected to fluctuate with changes in purchasing power and grow (or decline) with population rather than continue to expand with over-all increases in the standard of living. Clearly, the major consequence of such a change is that growth by any supplier can only be achieved at the expense of some other supplier, and market share becomes a much more meaningful indicator of performance than it is when the total market is expanding, as had been the case hitherto. In light of these changes, *Fortune* summarised the strategies of the Big Three in the following terms:

The briefest summary of future strategies is this: Ford and Chrysler place prime emphasis on a generally lower-priced market, which includes the compacts, and Ford is strongly impressed by the 'segmented' character of the overall market. General Motors appears much less committed to the new emphasis on the bottom of the price range. It seems to be pulling for the standard sized machine, and a rejuvenation of the middle-price brackets, with the compacts a fringe or supplemental market.

Elaborating on these themes, *Fortune* continues (in Robert McNamara's words): 'Ford's product strategy is based on a segmented market where different groups of consumers want different types of cars. We believe the general-purpose car will become a thing of the past; the expanding need is for specialised vehicles designed to fill a particular requirement.'

Like Ford, General Motors also recognised the concept of the segmented market but its problem was rather different than that faced by its old rival. The decline in G.M.s market share from 50.8 per cent in 1955 to 42.1 per cent in 1959 arose basically from a decline in demand for its middle-price makes, thus the prime strategic question facing the corporation was how it could move with the current trend toward cheaper, smaller cars with the least possible sacrifice of its Buick, Oldsmobile and Pontiac lines from which it derived most of its strength and profitability. In the end G.M. solved this dilemma by introducing a range of smaller cars with the Buick, Oldsmobile and Pontiac brand names but deliberately refrained from describing them as 'compacts'. *Fortune* continued

GM's strategy in essence, was to give the public what it wanted (i.e. smaller, cheaper, more economical cars) while at the same time trying to lead the buyers back to the standard-sized, middle-priced market, where GM still possessed so much competitive strength. Pointedly, GM refused to follow Ford's formula of concentrating on the lower-priced segments of the market with compacts and middle-priced cars at sharply reduced price tags. The GM strategy of going only part of the way down with the market was based on the hope that the 'man who had always wanted an Oldsmobile' (or Buick or Pontiac) would buy one of the new less expensive models and eventually trade up in the line, to the rejuvenation of the middle-priced market.

Chrysler adopted a strategy very similar to Ford's and increased its number of low-priced models. Clearly, its main objective was to remain a member of the Big Three rather than slip to join American Motors and Studebaker–Packard in a 'Little Three'.

In sum, the strategies of the Big Three stood both to help and hurt American Motors. By accepting the product features of compactness, durability and economy long promoted by American Motors, Ford, General Motors, and Chrysler had accepted a significant change in the nature of industry competition and were now competing on American Motors' home ground. On the other hand, while the increased selling and promotional efforts of the Big Three might be expected to stimulate primary demand for smaller, better-made and more economical cars, American Motors no longer enjoyed the distinction of being the only domestic producer offering these features. From holding a monopoly of a market segment they must now look forward to head-on competition from companies with significant advantages in production, marketing and distribution. How then did they fare during the 1960s?

AMERICAN MOTORS IN THE 1960s

During 1961 and 1962 American Motors sustained its 6 per cent market share and earned substantial profits but from then on its fortunes steadily declined.[8] In the authors' opinion this decline is largely attributable to the fact that the company persisted with its product policy which had been just right for market needs in 1958 but less so for the changing conditions of the early 1960s. An upturn in economic prosperity and a change in the leadership of the country had combined to emphasise youth, and this was reflected in the car market by a trend toward sporty cars, to high performance, and to extra accessories and options. Thus American Motors did not 'respond quickly' in the manner recommended in Chapter 3 when discussing marketing strategies for smaller companies.

1964 was the year of the Ford Mustang – the most success-ful new car ever with sales of 450,000 units in its first year of sales – and Chrysler also scored a marked success with its Barracuda – another sporty 'fastback' model. 'The trends toward "sportiness", and luxury, together with the large pro-liferation of models from 1962–1965, encouraged consumer buying up within the same brand. As a result, while 16·7 % of total car production in the 1962 model year fell in the $2,601–$3,100 price range, in the 1966 model year the figure had jumped to 33·7%.'[9] It will be recalled that this was just the effect which General Motors were seeking with their strategy.

George Romney had retired in 1962 to take up the gover-norship of Michigan and was succeeded by Roy Abernethy who held the reins until June 1966. Abernethy had worked under Romney and continued to try and sustain his predeces-sor's product policy while modifying it to reflect the changing needs of the market. The ambivalence implicit in this policy is well exemplified in Abernethy's briefing to his advertising agency: 'We build sporty cars, high performance cars, roomy cars, luxurious cars, stylish cars, *and* basic all-around economy cars . . . . But all will stay within our established design pre-cepts of trimness, manoeuvrability, efficiency and avoidance of excess.'[10]

Clearly, by attempting to pursue two different policies simultaneously – concentrated marketing with the compact car and undifferentiated marketing by seeking to establish a presence in every segment of the market like General Motors – Abernethy deprived American Motors of the single-minded-ness of purpose which had characterised its policy under Romney and ignored our dictum 'retreat when the enemy attacks' (Chapter 3).

In 1966 Robert Evans was elected as the next chairman. Evans was a financier who had acquired a large shareholding in American Motors. His comments clearly demonstrate his lack of understanding of the need for a product policy in keeping with an organisation's resources:

First, we must have fuller lines of cars that are at least as good as those of the Big Three and hopefully better. Next, we must have so-called personality cars, or glamour girls to appeal to all segments of the market. For example, we have been negligent of the youth market in the past. So we must now build cars that will excite youth, such as the AMX, which will be in the line next year, and other cars I can't discuss right now.

Abernethy resigned on 9 January 1967 and Evans followed him the next day. Roy D. Chapin, Jr, executive vice-president, was appointed chairman and chief executive and immediately instituted a survival strategy with four main objectives – raising cash, cutting costs, reducing break-even volume, and strengthening the dealerships – a remarkably similar strategy to that of Romney thirteen years previously. The similarity does not end there, for in his Report to the Stockholders published less than a month after taking up office Chapin commented:

We plan to direct ourselves more specifically to those areas of the market where we can be fully effective. We will use our resources where they count. We are not going to attempt to be all things to all people, but to concentrate on those areas of consumer needs we can meet better than anyone else. We believe the 'shotgun' approach to the general market is not for us, but instead we should take a rifle approach to specific segments of it. The spectacular success of the Rambler was largely due to an attack on a single unfulfilled part of the market. Today we intend to pick up the rifle again, although not in pursuit of one quarry but several, and provide a new freedom of choice.

By mid-1968 it appeared that Chapin's strategy (which accords well with our definition of differentiated marketing) might be going to work for it was noted that

The similarities between the factors affecting the auto market now and in the late 1950s are quite interesting. It will be recalled that at that time the prices of new U.S. autos were increasing to the point where they were out of the reach of many buyers. Foreign cars moved in to fill this vacuum and imports rose . . . George Romney capitalised on this by successfully promoting something different – the compact car. . . . The leading auto companies have again been increasing the prices of new autos. Again a void has been created. Once more imports have poured in to fill the vacuum, are now selling at an annual rate of one million units and are now accounting for over 10% of the U.S. market. . . . Whether history will repeat itself is a matter of speculation. Nevertheless the similarities are quite evident.[11]

In fact history did not repeat itself for American Motors, for 1968 was the year when the imported car first began to be recognised as a force to be reckoned with especially in the sub-compact segment. In 1969 sales of compact and sub-compact cars accounted for 22 per cent of all sales, 31 per cent in 1970, and 36 per cent in 1972. Over the same period imports rose from 11.24 to 19 per cent in 1973. To meet this flood, Ford introduced the Pinto, G.M. the Vega, and American Motors the Gremlin. 1971–2 sales are shown in Table 10.1.

TABLE 10.1   *U.S. automobile sales, 1971–2*

	1971	1972
Chevrolet Vega	345,161	332,646
Ford Pinto	340,756	456,561
American Gremlin	73,636	104,315
Volkswagen	522,655	485,617
Toyota	294,389	296,366
Datsun	188,029	192,707
Opel	88,535	69,407
Volvo	48,222	51,546
British Leyland	65,924	60,216
Capri (Ford)	56,118	91,464
Fiat	45,468	58,375
Mercedes Benz	31,115	36,306

Source: *Financial Times* (23 February 1973).

However, six years later, in 1974, history did in fact repeat itself. An article in the *Financial Times* went on to say that

'In stark contrast to the gloom enveloping the rest of the industry American Motors, the smallest of the Detroit manufacturers, had good news for its shareholders today. It reported
that its net operating profit rose by 22% in the final quarter of
last year and declared its first dividend since 1965.'[12]

Indeed the conditions in the U.S. market in 1973 were very
similar to those of 1957 when American Motors first recorded
a sales increase contrary to the general trend. While the downturn in the economy was compounded from a number of
causes, the Arab oil embargo and the ensuing 'energy crisis'
undoubtedly accounted for renewed interest in more economical cars.

SUMMARY

For the marketing strategist the fortunes of American Motors
raise a number of significant issues. Foremost among these
must be the question as to what product policy a small company should adopt when competing with firms very much
larger than itself. The evidence would seem to suggest that
one must seek a niche in the market which is sufficiently
attractive to keep one in profitable business but not sufficiently
large to attract the attention of the major producers.

The second major lesson which seems to emerge from the
case is that you should not let success go to your head. When
American Motors' niche in the market suddenly developed
into a major market segment due to change in environmental
forces the company seemed to lose focus. Instead of accepting
that the attention of the Big Three would boost primary
demand for compact cars to the extent that it would be possible to develop differentiated appeals within the segment,
American Motors took the attitude that it must compete with
the major producers across the whole range of models. Only
with the resignation of Abernethy and Evans did the company return to the philosophy expounded by George Romney of a 'rifle' rather than a 'shotgun' approach.

In the final analysis one cannot help but wonder about the
viability of a strategy which seems to owe so much to contra-
cyclical forces – when everyone else is down you are up. Over

a twenty-year period from 1954 to 1974 the evidence would seem to suggest that there were very few bad years in which economy was a prime buying motive and the Rambler car was perceived as a 'best buy'. If one takes a gloomy view of the future and feels that smaller, more economical cars are here to stay then it is clear that the major manufacturers will adjust their product policies accordingly. With a maximum lead time of three years for a new-model introduction one could hardly expect to enjoy the benefits of being in the right place at the right time with the right product for more than this period. Conversely, if the economy takes an upturn, can American Motors be sure of surviving the duration of the boom until the next recession brings the market back to its door?

Notes and References

CHAPTER 1

1. Ted Levitt, 'Marketing Myopia', *Harvard Business Review* (July–Aug 1960).
2. Maslow proposes that human needs exist on a number of levels ranked in order of priority, viz. Physiological, Safety, Belongingness and Love, Esteem and Status, Self-actualisation. Each level of need must be satisfied prior to the one below it in the hierarchy. Abraham H. Maslow, *Motivation and Personality* (New York: Harper & Row, 1954).
3. This is true even of planned economies. It is significant that consumers in the Soviet Union prefer to save a considerable proportion of their incomes rather than spend it on available consumer goods which have been produced without reference to their expressed needs.
4. Laurence Abbot, *Quality and Competition* (New York: Columbia University Press, 1955) p. 9.
5. Joan Robinson, *The Economics of Imperfect Competition* (London: Macmillan, 1932) and Edward Chamberlin, *The Theory of Monopolistic Competition* (Cambridge, Mass.: Harvard University Press, 1933).
6. The concept of market segmentation is developed in some detail in Chapter 3.
7. M. J. Baker, *Marketing New Industrial Products* (London: Macmillan, 1975).
8. Figures 1.3 and 1.4 are based on 'Experiences in Marketing Management', *The Marketing Executive Looks Ahead*, 13, National Industrial Conference Board (New York, 1967).

CHAPTER 2

1. National Economic Development Office, *A Handbook for Marketing Machinery* (London: H.M.S.O., 1940) p. 16.
2. Ibid.
3. P. J. Verdoorn, 'Marketing from the Producer's Point of View, *Journal of Marketing*, vol. 20, no. 2 (Jan 1956) pp. 49–56.

4. M. T. Cunningham and M. A. A. Hammouda, 'Product Planning in Engineering Companies: A Recent Research Survey', *British Journal of Marketing* (Summer 1969).

5. *Harvard Business School*, I.C.H. Order No. 4G98 (Intercollegiate Bibliography: Cases in Business Administration).

6. The machine-tool industry, to give an example, is heavily populated by firms of all sizes still bearing their founders' names. The influence of these men even today may be greater than is sometimes believed. Thus, in one case, managers spoke with affection of the founder, but expressed relief that they were at last beginning to shake off the worst effects of his influence. This man had retained a dominant interest in the company until a very old age. His approach to solving the company's problems of increasing competition and a short order book was, according to one senior executive in the company, 'lay down more lines and build more lathes'.

CHAPTER 3

1. See the works by Andrews, Ansoff and Bell cited at the end of the chapter (p. 44).

2. Neil H. Borden, 'The Concept of the Marketing Mix', in *Science in Marketing*, ed. George Schwartz (New York: Wiley, 1965).

3. M. J. Baker, *Marketing New Industrial Products* (London: Macmillan, 1975).

4. Hugo E. R. Uyterhoeven *et al.*, *Strategy and Organisation* (Homewood, Ill.: Irwin, 1973).

5. F. D. Boggis, 'Can you me-too?', in *Innovation in Marketing*, Proceedings of the Marketing Theory Seminar, ed. M. J. Baker (University of Strathclyde, 1974).

6. Robert L. Katz, *Management of the Total Enterprise* (Englewood Cliffs, N.J.: Prentice-Hall, 1970).

7. Philip Kotler, *Marketing Management*, 2nd edn (Englewood Cliffs, N.J.: Prentice-Hall, 1972) pp. 182–7.

8. Wendell R. Smith, 'Product Differentiation and Market Segmentation as Alternative Marketing Strategies', *Journal of Marketing*, vol. 21 (July 1956).

9. James F. Engel, Henry F. Fiorillo and Murray A. Cayley (eds) *Market Segmentation* (New York: Holt, Rinehart & Winston, 1972) p. 10. This section draws heavily on this source.

10. Ibid. p. 12.

11. *Market Management*.

12. The influence of behavioural factors in industrial buying decisions is the subject of detailed analysis in Baker, *Marketing New Industrial Products*, and of more general treatment in Frederick E. Webster, Jr and Yoram Wind, *Organisational Buying Behaviour* (Englewood Cliffs, N.J.: Prentice Hall, 1972).

13. Samuel C. Johnson and Conrad Jones, 'How to Organise New Products', *Harvard Business Review* (May–June 1957).

14. Thomas Staudt, 'Programme for Product Diversification', *Harvard Business Review* (Nov–Dec 1954).

CHAPTER 4

1. Martin L. Bell, *Marketing Concepts and Strategy* (London: Macmillan, 1966) p. 29.

2. For those seeking an extended treatment of such opportunities one can do no better than read Theodore Levitt's *Innovation in Marketing* (New York: McGraw-Hill, 1962).

3. T. Levitt, 'Innovative Imitation', *Harvard Business Review* (Sept–Oct 1966). See also the 'imitate' and 'adapt' strategies in Chapter 3.

4. Francis J. Aguilar, *Scanning the Business Environment* (New York: Macmillan, 1967).

5. Herman Kahn and Anthony J. Wiener, *The Year 2000* (London: Macmillan, 1967).

6. Erich Jantsch, 'Forecasting the Future', *Science Journal* (Oct 1967).

7. D. Meadows *et al.*, *Limits to Growth* (London: Earth Island, 1972).

8. Fritz Zwickey, *Monographs on Morphological Research*, Society for Morphological Research (Pasadena, 1962).

9. See Jantsch, 'Forecasting the Future'.

10. Thomas L. Berg and Abe Schuchman (eds), *Product Strategy and Management* (New York: Holt, Rinehart & Winston, 1963).

11. Ibid. pp. 146–72.

12. Ibid. ch. 14.

13. A. W. Frey (ed.), *Marketing Handbook*, 2nd edn (New York: Ronald Press, 1965).

14. The points are taken from M. J. Baker, *Marketing: An Introductory Text*, 2nd ed. (London: Macmillan, 1974).

15. Ibid.

16. Kotler, *Marketing Management*.

17. A detailed example of the application of the Bayesian approach to determining how much to spend on market research is to be found in Frank M. Bass 'Marketing Research Expenditures: A Decision Model', *Journal of Business* (Jan 1963).

CHAPTER 5

1. Joseph R. Mancuso, 'How to Manage Products', *Management Today* (Jan 1973).

2. B. Charles Ames, 'Pay-off from Product Management', *Harvard Business Review*, vol. 41 (Nov–Dec 1963).

3. 'The Marketing Manager – Gone Before He Arrives?' *Sales Management* (1 June 1969).

4. 'Has the Product Manager Failed?' *Sales Management* (1 Jan 1967).

5. 'The Product Manager System', *Experiences in Marketing Management*, no. 8 (N.I.C.B., 1965) p. 13.

6. D. J. Luck, 'Interfaces of a Product Manager', *Journal of Marketing*, vol. 33 (Oct 1969).

7. Ames, 'Pay-off from Product Management'.

8. Mancusco, 'How to Manage Products'.

9. W. S. Callander, 'Product Management and its Challenge to General Organization Concepts', *Proceedings* (Cincinnati. 1962) pp. 369–82.

10. 'Product Managers: Controversial Go-Getters', *Steel* features (21 Aug 1967).

11. Ames, 'Pay-off from Product Management', p. 143.

12. 'Has the Product Manager Failed? or The Folly of Imitation', (1 Jan 1967) pp. 27 ff.

13. D. J. Luck and T. Novak, 'Product Management – Vision Unfulfilled', *Harvard Business Review*, vol. 43 (May–June 1965).

14. Ames, 'Pay-off from Product Management'.

15. G. R. Gemmill and D. L. Wilemon, 'Interpersonal Barriers to Effective Product Management', *British Journal of Marketing* (Winter 1970–1).

16. Ibid. p. 209.

17. Ibid. pp. 213–14.

18. P. R. Lawrence and J. W. Lorsch, 'New Management Job: The Integrator', *Harvard Business Review* (Nov Dec 1967).

19. Ames, 'Pay-off from Product Management'; Luck, 'Interfaces of a Product Manager'; Luck and Novak, 'Product Management – Vision Unfulfilled'.

20. Ames, 'Pay-off from Product Management'.

21. Luck, 'Interfaces of a Product Manager'.

CHAPTER 6

1. L. Cooklin, 'Case Study' in *New Product Development*, ed. D. Roxburgh, Conference Proceedings, University of Strathclyde (Mar 1966) p. 135. Cooklin is marketing director of a consultancy firm whose experience of assisting companies with new product development is considerable. He stresses that, although the classification appears somewhat rigid at first, his experience is that its use 'can be very worthwhile', though a degree of flexibility is required in its application.

2. Booz, Allen and Hamilton, *Management of New Products* (New York: 1960).

3. E. A. Pessemier, *New Product Decisions: An Analytical Approach* (New York: McGraw-Hill, 1966) p. 40.

4. Ibid. ch. 4 especially. In considering a situation where the decision is to scrap the product or add it to the product line, Pessemier suggests that 'the proposed new product will be dropped' where the 'best alternative' is expected to yield a return below the company's opportunity cost of capital, thus assuming a kind of automatic management reaction.

5. C. Berenson, 'The R & D: Marketing Interface – A General Analogue Model for Technology Diffusion', *Journal of Marketing*, vol. 32, no. 2 (Apr 1968).

6. H. I. Ansoff and J. M. Stewart, 'Strategies for a technology-based business', in *The Arts of Top Management*, ed. R. Mann (New York: McGraw-Hill, 1970).

7. P. R. Lawrence and J. W. Lorsch, *Organisation and Environment* (Homewood, Ill.: Irwin, 1969).

8. E. P. Ward, *The Dynamics of Planning* (London: Pergamon Press, 1970).

9. T. Levitt, *The Marketing Mode* (New York: McGraw-Hill 1969) pp. 129–55.

10. The figure is from Ward, *The Dynamics of Planning*, p. 300.

11. D. A. Schon, *Technology and Change* (Delacorte Press, 1967).

12. *Measuring, Directing and Controlling New Product Development*, Industrial and Commercial Techniques Ltd (May 1968).

13. T. Burns, *The Innovative Process and the Organization of Industrial Science*, in Main Speeches Conference Papers, European

Industrial Research Management Association, vol. 5 (Paris, 1967).

14. M. Shanks, *The Innovators* (Harmondsworth: Penguin, 1967) p. 64.

15. See, for example, 'Start More Little Businesses and More Little Businessmen', *Innovation*, no. 5 (1969); also Mackhanan, 'Corporate Growth through Venture Management', *Harvard Business Review* (Jan–Feb 1969).

CHAPTER 7

1. Sir Alec Cairncross, Presidential address to the British Association, delivered 1 September 1971.

2. See, for example, E. F. Brech, C. de Paula and N. White, *Management of Research and Development: A Symposium*, British Institute of Management (1964) and, E. D. Reeves, *Management of Industrial Research* (New York: Reinhold, 1967).

3. D. Allison (ed.), *The R & D Game* (Massachusetts Institute of Technology Press, 1969) p. 169.

4. H. B. G. Casimir, 'G. Holst: Profile of a Research Director', *Science Journal*, vol. 5A, no. 1 (July 1969).

5. Tom Burns and G. M. Stalker, *The Management of Innovation*, (London: Tavistock, 1961).

6. D. W. Karger and R. G. Murdick, *New Product Venture Management* (New York: Gordon & Breach, 1972) p. 79.

7. Ibid. p. 79.

8. Ward, *The Dynamics of Planning*, p. 121.

9. D. W. Foster, *Planning for Products and Markets* (London: Longmans, 1972).

10. Karger and Murdick, *New Product Venture Management*, pp. 81–6.

11. R. M. Hill, R. S. Alexander, and J. S. Cross, *Industrial Marketing*, 4th edn (Homewood, Ill.: Irwin, 1975).

12. Ward, *The Dynamics of Planning*, p. 143.

13. Karger and Murdick, *New Product Venture Management*, p. 83.

14. Ward, *The Dynamics of Planning*, p. 130.

15. See 'the imitation of strategy' discussed in Chapter 3.

16. B. R. Williams, 'Information and Criteria in Capital Expenditure Decisions', *Journal of Management Studies* (Sept 1964).

17. J. Olin, *R and D Management Practices: Chemical Industry in Europe* (Zürich: Stanford Research Institute, 1972).

18. C. Freeman, *The Economics of Industrial Innovation* (Harmondsworth: Penguin, 1974) p. 328.

19. A. Wilson, 'Selecting New Products for Development', *Scientific Business* (Nov 1963).

20. The reader may wish to refer back to our remarks on resource auditing in Chapter 4 to give added perspective to this point.

21. Wilson, 'Selecting New Products for Development'.

22. For a description of such methods see A. R. Toll, 'New Techniques in Product Planning', in *New Ideas in Industrial Marketing*, eds T. C. Coram and R. W. Hill (London: Staple Press, 1970).

23. Freeman, *The Economics of Industrial Innovation*, p. 240.

24. A. Hart, 'A Chart for Evaluating Product R & D Projects', *Operational Research Quarterly*, vol. 17, no. 4 (1966) pp. 347–58.

CHAPTER 8

1. M. Asimow, *Introduction to Design* (Englewood Cliffs, N.J.: Prentice-Hall, 1962).

2. G. B. R. Feilden, *Engineering Design*, Report of a Committee appointed by the Council for Scientific and Industrial Research to consider the present standing of Mechanical Engineering Design, Department of Scientific and Industrial Research (13 June 1963).

3. R. L. Willsmer, in an address to senior executives of the Thompson Organisation at Strathclyde University (29 April 1971).

4. D. W. Ewing, 'Corporate Planning at a Crossroads', *Harvard Business Review* (July–Aug 1967).

5. The case described here is that of the Cambridge Instrument Co. Ltd. For further details of the company's outlook and practices see P. Goudime, 'An Instrument Company's Approach to the Management of Research and Development', in *Innovation for Profit*, Scientific Instrument Research Association, Adam Higher Ltd (London, 1968).

6. Asimow, *Introduction to Design*, p. 28.

7. Ewing, 'Corporate Planning at a Crossroads'.

8. Schon, *Technology and Change*, p. 65.

9. G. Broadbent, 'A Plain Man's Guide to Systematic Design Methods', *Royal Institute of British Architects' Journal* (May 1968).

10. Ewing, 'Corporate Planning at a Crossroads', p. 84.

11. Asimow, *Introduction to Design*, p. 26.

12. The case described is in effect a plea for 'organic' rather than 'mechanistic' organisation structures, as described by Burns and Stalker, *The Management of Innovation*, pp. 119–22. A

characteristic of the organic structure is the importance of lateral communications through the organisation, this facilitating discussions across departmental boundaries, in contrast with the hierarchic structure emphasising vertical interaction typical of the mechanistic organisation arrangement. The latter is clearly inimical to an integrated design approach.

13. This case can be studied in greater detail in S. S. Carlisle, 'Case Studies in Product Development', paper read at the second International Conference on Product Development and Manufacturing Technology, University of Strathclyde (April 1971).

14. E. G. Malmlow, 'Corporate Strategic Planning in Practice', *Long Range Planning*, vol. 5, no. 3 (Sept 1972) pp. 2–9.

CHAPTER 9

1. P. Iff, 'New Product Concept Testing', in *Seminar on Research for New Product Development* (ESOMAR, 1970).

2. Ibid. p. 49.

3. Ibid. p. 51.

4. Ibid. p. 52.

5. For more details on this and other aspects of market testing see 'Market Testing Consumer Products', *Experiences in Marketing Management*, no. 12, National Industrial Conference Board (New York: 1967) pp. 44–59.

6. For more details of the use of concept testing in industrial markets, see M. B. MacDonald, Jr, *Appraising the Market for New Industrial Products*, Business Policy Study No. 123, National Industrial Conference Board (New York, 1967).

7. Iff, 'New Product Concept Testing', p. 52.

8. J. C. Penny, I. M. Hunt and W. A. Twyman, 'Product testing methodology in relation to marketing problems – a review', *Journal of the Market Research Society*, vol. 14, no. 1 (Jan 1972).

9. Dr Jorg Rehorn, 'Product tested – what then? Five decision aids for assessing test results', *European Research*, vol. 2, no. 3 (May 1974).

10. Penny, *et al.* 'Product testing methodology in relation to marketing problems', seek to assess subjective experience in the product test.

11. L. W. Rodger, *Marketing in a Competitive Economy* (London: Hutchinson, 1965) p. 123.

12. John Davis, 'The Validity of Test Marketing', *Commentary*, vol. VII, no. 3 (July 1965).

13. *How to strengthen your product plan*, A. C. Nielsen Co Ltd, Oxford (undated).

14. Ibid. p. 18.

15. Rodger, *Marketing in a Competitive Economy* pp. 126–7.

16. Davis, 'The Validity of Test Marketing'.

17. 'Over half new products still fail', *Financial Times* (15 Feb 1973).

18. See 'Cadbury launches first soup', *Financial Times* (8 Nov 1973).

19. Baker, *Marketing New Industrial Products*.

20. Ibid.

21. R. S. Alexander, 'The Death and Burial of "Sick" Products', *Journal of Marketing*, vol. 28, no. 2 (Apr 1964) pp. 1–7.

22. See, for example, A. H. Taylor, *Costing: a Management Approach* (London: Pan Books, 1974).

23. Alexander, 'The Death and Burial of "Sick" Products'.

24. Baker, *Marketing New Industrial Products*.

CHAPTER 10

1. The case study number being BP765.

2. Alfred P. Sloan Jr, *My Years with General Motors*, ed. John McDonald with Catherine Stevens (London: Pan Books, 1963).

3. Ibid. p. 89.

4. Ibid. p. 92.

5. The Tobe Lectures in Retail Distribution, Harvard Business School, 1958–9.

6. Course BP765.

7. Ibid.

8. A description covering the period to 1968 is to be found in American Motors Corporation (E), BP907, Harvard Business School.

9. Ibid.

10. Ibid.

11. *The Wall Street Transcript* (29 April 1968).

12. 'American Motors reverses trend', *Financial Times* (7 Feb 1974).

Index